How To Master in **Human Psychology**

Introduction

Since you have got a lot of insights into reading other people's personality; let us tell you why you need to analyze people and what is the significance of it.

Body language is a universal language. Almost all of us use body signs for non-verbal communication with others. The ability to understand body language is perhaps one of the most valuable tools you can possess in understanding others. When you understand what's really being communicated to you, it takes the conversation to a whole new level. You're able to make people feel at ease. You're easily able to establish a deep sense of rapport. You also become likeable. All of these things are extremely useful to you because ultimately people like giving their love, support, business what've you to people that they like.

The bottom line: The more you understand another persons thoughts, feelings, needs, the more you can actually relay back to them what they need to get from you. The more you're able to relate to them, the more likeable you become. The more likeable you become, the more you're able to get what you want.

Understanding body language isn't really difficult once you know the basics. It's sort of like learning a new language though, in that you're learning what different gestures & expression mean.

Understanding body language is used in a lot of different professions. Usually, police officers are given some training in understanding body language as it's useful when interrogating a suspect or while talking to a witness. By using the other person's body language, the officer can also easily determine whether the person is telling the truth.

Understanding body language is also quite essential when it comes to the education profession. Especially with children, it's vital for teacher to have an understanding of body language. Usually, kids aren't fully capable of expressing their feelings using their vocabulary. Therefore, educators should've a basic understanding of body language in order to fully grasp what their students are trying to communicate.

When it comes to giving commands or even conveying messages, understanding body language plays a key role. If the people with whom you work or even interact with also have an understanding of body language, then it's quite easy for you to communicate with them. Additionally, the right combination of body language & verbal communication can also produce more effective communication.

Understanding body language usually helps a person to easily portray her or his personality. There may be people you know of in your life that you've perhaps never actually had a conversation with, but you still can get a vague idea of how they actually operate based on watching their nonverbal expression. This's that energy vibration you pick up on, when you know someone's in a bad mood or a good mood. You feel it somehow without them saying a word.

But, it's also due to the very fact that your subconscious mind already understands & interprets body language. & your subconscious mind sends you that information it knows through your feelings you get about another person. You also don't' necessarily know on a conscious level why you actually feel the way you about them, but you know, there's just something about them that you either want to experience more of or perhaps something that you want to avoid being around.

This book contains proven steps & strategies on how to interpret & use body language to communicate without relying solely on verbal & vocal cues.

You'll learn about tips & techniques to better understand how other people are really feeling on top of what they're saying. There're also tricks to help you control how others perceive you to your advantage.

Introduction to visual communication

Body language points to the nonverbal cues employed by humans to possess effective communication with one another. Such nonverbal signals, consistent with scholars, constitute a serious part of daily interaction. The things we don't say can still transmit amounts of data from our visual communication to our physical movements. It's also been reported that visual communication can account for about 60 per cent and 65 per cent of all communication. It's necessary to know visual communication, and it's vital to pay close attention to other signals like meaning. In many situations, rather than counting on one event, you want to check out signals as a band. Once you learn and master the way to use visual communication for effective communication, you'll even be ready to manipulate individuals psychologically during a positive manner. This chapter will expound more on the definition and aspects of visual communication. Allow us to start.

What is body language?

Even once they don't express their opinions verbally, the bulk still miss clues about what they think and feel. Non-verbal signals transmitted through the formation of the sender's body, physical appearance, voice inflexions and intensity of the voice and various signs are all mentioned as non-verbal communication.

Non-verbal communication is typically not as simple because it is conveyed in words, but how it's expressed could combat a serious job by recognizing somebody and interfacing with others. It is a quiet ensemble: miniexpressions (short presentations of feeling that individual attempts to disguise), hand gestures, and therefore the recording of posture within the human mind very rapidly in any event, when someone isn't consciously conscious of them.

These acknowledgement snapshots, however short, can have lasting repercussions on how a private translates the inspiration, disposition, and receptivity of others also as how they see their own inner identity. Regrettably, certain psychological well-being issues, particularly neuropsychiatric issues like a mental defect, may make it, even more, trying to check to acknowledge and answer non-verbal communication messages.

Types of visual communication

There are sorts of visual communication. This is often because we cannot classify the various styles within the same category. Different body languages are often distinguished. So, which visual communication styles are often differentiated? Generally, visual communication is split into two columns. That has body parts and therefore the intent.

So what kinds in each class are often observed?

Let us start with the body parts and therefore the language they convey.

The head - the location of the top and its movement, back and forth, right to left, side to side, and therefore the shake of hair.

Face - this includes facial expressions. You ought to note that the face has many muscles starting from 54 to 98 whose work is to man oeuvre different areas of the face. The movements of the face depict the state of your mind.

Eyebrows - the eyebrows can express themselves through moving up and down, also as giving a frown.

Eyes - the eyes are often rolled, move up and down, right and left, blink and dilate.

The nose - the expression of the nose is often by the flaring of the nostrils and therefore the formation of wrinkles at the highest.

The lips - there are many roles played by the lips, they include snarling, smiling, kissing, opened, closed, tight, and puckering

The tongue - the tongue can appear and out, go up and down, touch while kissing, and also the licking of lips.

The jaw - the jaw opens and closes. It is often clinched, and therefore the mandible is often moved right and left also.

Your body posture - this describes the way you place your body, legs, and arms altogether, and also in relation with people.

The body proximity - this looks at how far or near your body is to people.

Shoulder movements - they move up and down, get hunched, and hung.

The arm - these go up and down, straight and cross

The legs and feet - these can have an expression in many various ways. They will be straight, crossed, one leg placed over the opposite, the feet facing the subsequent person you're during a conversation with, or face faraway from one another, the feet are often dangling the shoes than on.

The hand and therefore the fingers - the way that your hands and fingers move is powerful in reading other people's gestures. The hands can move up and down or do some hidden language that only people of an equivalent group can understand.

Handling and placing of objects reaction by one - this is often not considered apart, but it technically plays a task in reading visual communication. This might predict anger, happiness and far more.

Moreover, this includes willingly making body movements otherwise referred to as gestures. They're the movements that you simply shall make. For instance, shaking of hands, blinking of the eyes, moving and shaking the body during a sexy way, maybe to lure someone and far more.

There also are involuntary movements- the movements that you simply haven't any control over. It is often sweating, laughter, crying and far more. Further, in chapter two, we shall expound more on the body parts and what each expression means.

Importance of visual communication

Most individuals believe social networks and texts to attach during this modern digital age, and it's a really reliable way for doing so.

While data communication enables people to talk at convenience and may reduce stress on certain individuals, something are often lost in so doing, and since you're incapable of recognizing the person once you speak to them, you'll misconstrue non-verbal signs to verbal ones like vocal inflexions. Data communication has become the most method for people around the world, and to satisfy this fact, there's the likelihood that visual communication will proceed to develop. Most of the time, you'll hear the pessimistic a part of visual communication. Maybe you were told to not twist during a certain way, sit this manner or that way. However, visual communication can influence your life positively. Allow us to check out what you ought to do to maximize visual communication.

How visual communication can influence effective communication

Well, we may feel and need that interaction is as easy because the phrases that we are saying, it's not the reality. The truth is that our message is heard quite just our words. If in an email, text, or instant message, you have ever been mistaken for somebody else, you recognize what I'm talking about. Words alone aren't enough. The visual communication is a component of what strengthens and wraps up the message. So, if individuals see us faceto-face or using video cameras, our visual communication influences our message and presentation. You'll find that visual communication helps the receiver of data, read your mind and interpret your thoughts. Acknowledge that there is more to the message that you're sending, there's the metamessage of who you're and therefore the intention to send that message. Visual communication is consistently communicating with your audience.

Nonetheless, my aim during this is to supply you some specific advice to assist your communication within the visual communication that you simply use, and to extend the probabilities that your message are going to be heard and understood properly.

Always make eye contact

It is first on the list, without a doubt. You'll be surprised to notice that, our eyes talk more on our behalf. However, this is often susceptible to some cultural differences. We develop confidence in what we are saying and believe the opposite individual once we make eye contact. Our eyes could also be the portals to our soul, but they're certainly how to develop a relationship and supply effective communication. You'll say that you simply are shy and unable to form eye contact most of the time. Well, the shyness may cause you to seem down or sideways while communicating. Your audience may interpret this as a scarcity of confidence in your message.

This is often why it's important to nurture your eye contact. The great thing about visual communication is that you simply can learn it with time. Start developing talents gradually.

Walk energetically

Picture the primary time you meet anyone. During a sluggish posture, they are available to you, ambling towards you. Picture an equivalent scenario now with a private walking with intent and power–we're not brooding about sprinting, but a deliberate walk. This mere act is that the individual's opinion, isn't it? Our walking style sends out a message of trust and authenticity to people around us and may additionally portray beauty. Once you enter confidence, you depict that you simply know what you're up to and believe yourself. You recognize what happens next; people will believe you too.

Bring out a mirrored image

Our feelings and considerations appear through our non-verbal communication, which is the purpose of this text. Once you got to discuss better with others, consider reflecting their non-verbal communication. This is not a YouTube snapshot of an infant emulating another person, the very fact of the matter isn't to repeat or ridicule somebody, but to point out sympathy through your non-verbal communication. This must be inconspicuous and can take practice. However, it can enable your messages to be gotten all the more effectively by others.

Give individuals an opportunity to ascertain their hands

We, as an entire, utilize our hands to convey a message. You'll even watch individuals on the phone, utilizing their hands to present their meaningful conclusion, while the opposite individual can't in any way, shape or see them! At the purpose when individuals can't see our hands, they wonder on the off chance that we are concealing something, maybe we are anxious, or other numerous things. Your hands are a bit of your effective communication; so, use them and maintain a strategic distance from any negatives which will originate from concealing them from others.

Utilize empowering non-verbal communication

Two quick models: one-to-one connection is referenced as of now, and gesturing with individuals to point out that you simply comprehend and concur also. When somebody does that, it conveys being capable to you, isn't it? This is not the most model. Identified with reflecting over utilizes our body development and motions to point out individuals that we provide it with a reconsideration and wish to tune to realize from them, which what we are sharing is to their greatest advantage also.

Slow down

A few folks speed up our communication. It's advisable to hamper. However, it hinders your signals and development. While some speed conveys vitality, there are some negligible differences that we cross and these give room for our non-verbal communication to point out tension, apprehension, or maybe contemptibility. Take a full breath and relax a touch bit.

Have a fantastic handshake

If you've got one, you'll realize how significant this is often. If you're unconscious of this reality, you would possibly just have a limp, dead fish, or overwhelming and over-controlling handshake. A handshake communicates something specific about what your identity is. Work on a firm, don't hesitate to welcome handshake and you'll impart believability and certainty to people.

Furthermore, we as an entire can and will affect this stuff. We'd like to perceive that the beneficiary of our message, the watcher of our non-verbal communication, is that the judge. Their view of our non-verbal communication runs the day. At the purpose, once we apply the thoughts above, however, we'll improve the chances that their discernment is for certain and can bolster better correspondences and connections.

Here are more powerful tips and their relevance in communication

To enhance your confidence, undertake the facility pose

Research shows that really holding your body in broad, high-powered poses that involve leaning back together with your arms behind your feet and head on your chair, or standing together with your arms and legs wide open for as little as two minutes promotes higher levels of testosterone, a hormone connected to dominance and power. Do that when you're getting nervous but want to seem confident. Such positions, additionally to triggering hormonal changes in both males and females cause a rise in the emotion of dominance and better risk perception.

Act like you're taking note of encourage participation

If you would like your audience to require action, don't multitask while they're doing it. Don't be tempted to see your SMS messages, to see the time, or see how the opposite members respond. Alternatively, by moving your head and body to face them directly and making eye contact, you'll consider those that are speaking. Leaning forward, nodding, and rotating your head are other ways to demonstrate your commitment and a spotlight through visual communication. Hearing people out is important. Being sure they understand that you simply are an attentive listener is simply as critical.

Get obviate barriers to possess a connection

To promote cooperation, remove everything that forestalls your vision or creates a wall for you and therefore the remainder of the group. Whilst you're taking a breather, be mindful that by keeping your teacup during a style that seems to shield your body intentionally or separate you from everyone else, you'll form a barrier. A senior executive once observed that the upper they kept their coffee cups, the better for him to work out the satisfaction of his staff. To rate the nervousness of the individuals, they have a tendency to carry their coffee cups at a high position. People that held at waist level with their hands were more relaxed than those with high chest and arms were.

Shake hands to create a connection

The act of touching has been considered the foremost powerful non-verbal cue to make an excellent reference to people... Touching others for just a couple of seconds on the arm, side, or shoulder, establishes a person's internal connection. Watching the workplace, through the handshake tradition, bodily touch and luxury are developed, and this tactile contact gives an enduring and positive feeling. Handshake research showed that if you shook hands with people, you're twice as likely to recollect them after you allow. Research has shown that folks are more open and friendly to the people they meet and greet with.

Smile to stimulate good feelings

A genuine smile doesn't only trigger your sense of well-being but also tells those around you that you simply are accessible, supportive, and reliable. A true smile slowly emerges, crinkles the eyes, and widens the lips, shines up the face, and slowly fades away. Most importantly, a smile features a direct impact on how others relate to you. You'll have noticed that once you smile at someone, they respond with a smile. Facial expressions have how of triggering more feelings related to the smile. Once you revisit a smile, it transforms the spirit of the opposite person in post-trigger corresponding feelings; the smile that you simply revisit actually changes the spirit of that person positively.

When in agreement, always show through expressions and therefore the posture

When clients or business partners unintentionally mimic your visual communication, it's their way of stating what proportion they like or suits you during a non-verbal manner. It is often an important part of developing relationships and fostering shared sentiments once you mirror other individuals with purpose. Mirroring begins by examining the gestures of an individual's face and body, then allowing your body to require similar statements and poses consciously. The opposite person will feel recognized and welcomed to try to so.

Always watch people's feet if you would like to find out the reality

As individuals attempt to regulate their expression of the body, they focus mainly on facial expressions, postures of the body, and movements of the hand/arm. Are often "> this is often because their feet and legs haven't been rehearsed; they're where all the truth can be identified commonly. By enhanced foot motions, individuals will often show anxiety and discomfort while undergoing any sort of stress. The feet will always fidget together around the seat. The feet can spread and curl to ease tension, and even leap out to escape during a remotely controlled effort. Studies have found that viewers are simpler in determining the important spirit of a private as they see the entire body. Maybe you do not know, but you've got been reacting to feet gestures all of your life.

Keep your voice right down to command authority

As you propose to form or receive a call alternatively a speech, you ought to let your voice relax into its optimal pitch. You'll achieve this by putting your lips together and make the voices of 'um, um hum'. Also, note that your voice doesn't go so high at the top of the sentences. It's going to be confused with asking questions or trying to hunt approval. To counter this, if you would like to state an opinion, use the authoritative pitch that starts with a coffee note and raises the voice throughout the sentence, but the voice goes down towards the top again. Once you adopt this, you'll be ready to take hold and command authority in each space.

Don't cross your legs; you'll enhance your memory

According to a study, people during a classroom who had unfolded legs and arms recorded a better memory of quite 35 per cent compared to those that had crossed them. Therefore, to reinforce your retention of data, you ought to unfold your arms and legs. If you're making a presentation and discovered these characteristics among your audience, change your strategy and do something which will enhance their listening. You'll take an opportunity and confirm that a change takes place by making them open and relax for concentration.

Will visual communication improve my life?

After getting the ideas, you'll be asking yourself whether indeed visual communication influences your life positively. I'm here to convince you that indeed, your life is sure to transform if you're taking some time to nurture your visual communication and its relevance in whatsoever thing that you simply do. You ought to know what to use at the proper time, were to be organized and articulate. This book will specialize in positive visual communication. That has good eye contact, effective engagement, targeted gestures that make your message more comprehensible and effective. In essence, visual communication has been found to make and enhance your confidence, influence, and all-round success. More studies have revealed that the people that skills to use their visual communication are more likeable, persuasive, competent, and possess a high level of emotional intelligence. This simply means they will command presence, manipulate their way into various platforms, and win people's hearts.

Positive non-verbal communication changes your frame of mind. From the research found that deliberately changing your non-verbal communication to form it increasingly positive, improves your demeanor since it powerfully affects your hormones.

It results in a rise in testosterone. At the purpose, once you hear of testosterone, your mind can easily be swayed to specialize in athletics, yet testosterone's significance covers substantially quite games. No matter whether you're a person or a woman, testosterone improves your certainty and makes other individuals consider you to be progressively dependable and positive. Research has shown that positive non-verbal communication builds your testosterone level by 20%.

In addition, visual communication results in a discount of cortisol. Cortisol may be a pressure hormone that blocks execution and makes negative wellbeing impacts over the end of the day. Reduction of cortisol level limits pressure and empowers you to think better, especially in troublesome and testing circumstances. Research shows that positive non-verbal communication diminishes the cortisol level by 25%.

It makes a groundbreaking blend. While a discount in cortisol and a rise in testosterone are incredible in their special ways, both are a groundbreaking blend that's normally observed among individuals in high positions. This blend makes the knowledge and clearness of mind that are perfect for managing tight deadlines, intense choices, and large amounts of labor. Individuals who normally have high testosterone and low level of cortisol are known to flourish struggling. Indeed, you'll utilize positive non-verbal communication to form yourself like this, no matter whether it does or doesn't occur normally.

Apart from that, it causes you to progressively attractive and likeable. During a study during a university, students watched soundless videos of doctors interacting with their patients. Just by watching the doctors' nonverbal communication, the scholars could conclude that the doctors would find yourself being sued by their patients. Non-verbal communication is a huge factor by the way you're seen and maybe a better priority than your manner of speaking or maybe what you state. Deciding the way to utilize constructive use of visual communication will make individuals believe in you, such as you and trust you more.

Moreover, it shows capability. In an investigation, scientists found that a one-second video of candidates during a campaign was ready to pinpoint the potential candidate that was voted for. This was possible due to their visual communication. Although this might not build your confidence within the democratic procedure, it shows that the view of capability features a solid establishment in non-verbal communication.

Finally, visual communication improves emotional intelligence. Your capacity to viably convey your feelings and thoughts is significant to your passionate knowledge. Individuals whose non-verbal communication is negative have a dangerous, infectious impact on everyone around them. Attempting to enhance your non-verbal communication profoundly affects your emotional intelligence.

What is nonverbal communication and body language?

Nonverbal communication will be communication without utilizing words – straightforward. Body language is a part of this communication concentrating chiefly on the distinctive body gestures and outward appearances.

At start it doesn't look like a lot – how might somebody say anything without utilizing words? Would you be able to state "I love elephants" without verbalizing it?

In any case, clearly there is a lot to be said from the implied. All kind of data can be accumulated from:

- Facial expressions
- Gestures
- Posture
- Touch
- Tone of voice
- Rate of discourse
- Volume of voice • Physical appearance
- Stress of voice
- Personal space
- Clothes
-
-
-

- Hair style
- Hygiene
- Engagement with others, (for example, to what extent do you keep eye contact)

For what reason does nonverbal communication make a difference?

Your nonverbal communication signs—the manner in which you tune in, look, move, and respond—tell the individual you're speaking with whether you give it a second thought, in case you're being honest, and how well you're tuning in. At the point when your nonverbal signals coordinate with the words you're stating, they increment trust, clearness, and affinity.

At the point when they don't, they can create pressure, question, and disarray.

On the other hand

that you need to improve as a communicator, it's critical to turn out to be progressively touchy not exclusively to the body language and nonverbal signals of others, yet in addition to your own.

Nonverbal communication can assume five jobs:

Repetition: It rehashes and frequently reinforces the message you're making verbally.

Contradiction: It can repudiate the message you're attempting to pass on, in this way showing to your audience that you may not be coming clean.

Substitution: It can fill in for a verbal message. For instance, your outward appearance regularly passes on an undeniably more striking message than words ever can.

Complementing: It might add to or supplement your verbal message.

As a chief, on the off chance that you pat a worker on the back notwithstanding giving recognition, it can build the effect of your message.

Accenting: It might highlight or underline a verbal message. Beating the table, for instance, can underline the significance of your message.

- Sorts of nonverbal communication
- Here are nine sorts of nonverbal signals and
- practices: Outward appearances

Outward appearances are answerable for a tremendous extent of nonverbal communication. Consider how much data can be conveyed with a grin or a glare. The expression on an individual's face is frequently the primary thing we see, even before we hear what they need to state.

While nonverbal communication and conduct can differ drastically between cultures, the outward appearances for bliss, sadness, outrage, and dread are comparative all through the world.

Gestures
Conscious developments and signals are a significant method to impart importance without words. Basic gestures incorporate waving, pointing, and utilizing fingers to demonstrate numeric sums. Different gestures are subjective and identified with culture.

In court settings, attorneys have been known to use distinctive nonverbal signals to endeavor to influence legal hearer feelings. A lawyer may look at his watch to propose that the restricting legal advisor's contention is repetitive or may even feign exacerbation at the declaration offered by an observer trying to undermine their believability. These nonverbal signals are viewed as being so incredible and powerful that a few judges even spot confines on what sort of nonverbal practices are permitted in the court.

Paralinguistic

Paralinguistic alludes to vocal communication that is independent from real language. This incorporates factors, for example, manner of speaking, din, enunciation, and pitch. Consider the amazing impact that manner of speaking can have on the significance of a sentence. When said in a solid manner of speaking, audience members may decipher endorsement and eagerness. Similar words said in a reluctant manner of speaking may pass on objection and an absence of intrigue.

Consider all the various ways that just changing your manner of speaking may change the importance of a sentence. A companion may ask you how you are getting along, and you may react with the standard "I'm fine," however how you really state those words may uncover an enormous measure of how you are truly feeling.

A virus manner of speaking may recommend that you are really not fine, however you don't wish to examine it. A splendid, happy manner of speaking will uncover that you are really doing very well. A serious, dejected tone would demonstrate that you are something contrary to fine and that maybe your companion ought to ask further.

Body Language and Posture

Posture and development can likewise pass on a lot of data. Body language has developed essentially since the 1970s, yet famous media have concentrated on the over-translation of cautious postures, arm-intersection, and leg-crossing.

While these nonverbal practices can demonstrate emotions and frames of mind, investigate proposes that body language is unmistakably more unobtrusive and less authoritative than recently accepted.

Proxemics

Individuals frequently allude to their requirement for "individual space," which is additionally a significant sort of nonverbal communication. The measure of distance we need and the measure of room we see as having a place with us is impacted by various variables including social standards, social desires, situational factors, character qualities, and level of recognition.

For instance, the measure of individual space required when having an easygoing discussion with someone else as a rule fluctuates between 18 crawls to four feet. Then again, the individual distance required when addressing a horde of individuals is around 10 to 12 feet.

Eye Gaze

The eyes assume a significant job in nonverbal communication and such things as looking, gazing and squinting are significant nonverbal practices. At the point when individuals experience individuals or things that they like, the pace of squinting increments and understudies enlarge. Taking a gander at someone else can show a scope of feelings including threatening vibe, intrigue, and fascination.

Individuals additionally use eye gaze as a way to decide whether somebody is being straightforward. Ordinary, watchful gaze contact is frequently taken as a sign that an individual is coming clean and is reliable. Tricky eyes and a failure to keep in touch, then again, is regularly observed as a marker that somebody is lying or being misleading.

Haptics

Imparting through touch is another significant nonverbal conduct. There has been a significant measure of research on the significance of touch in early stages and early adolescence.

How denied touch and contact obstructs advancement. Infant monkeys raised by wire moms experienced changeless deficiencies in conduct and social communication. Contact can be utilized to convey fondness, recognition, compassion, and different feelings.

Contact is additionally frequently utilized as an approach to convey both status and force. High-status people will in general attack others' close to home space with more prominent recurrence and force than lower-status people. Sex contrasts likewise assume a job in how individuals use contact to impart meaning.

Ladies will in general use contact to pass on care, concern, and nurturance. Men, then again, are bound to utilize contact to attest force or command over others.

Appearance
Our decision of shading, dress, haircuts, and different variables influencing appearance are likewise viewed as a methods for nonverbal communication. Shading psychology has exhibited that various hues can bring out various states of mind. Appearance can likewise change physiological responses, decisions, and understandings.

Simply think about all the inconspicuous decisions you rapidly make about somebody dependent on their appearance. These early introductions are significant, which is the reason specialists propose that activity searchers dress properly for interviews with potential businesses.

Specialists have discovered that appearance can assume a job in how individuals are seen and even the amount they acquire. Lawyers who were evaluated as more appealing than their friends earned almost 15 percent more than those positioned as less alluring.

Antiques

Items and pictures are additionally apparatuses that can be utilized to impart nonverbally. On an online discussion, for instance, you may choose a symbol to speak to your character on the web and to impart data about what your identity is and the things you like. Individuals regularly invest a lot of energy building up a specific picture and encircle themselves with objects intended to pass on data about the things that are imperative to them.

Garbs, for instance, can be utilized to transmit an enormous measure of data about an individual. A warrior will wear exhausts, a cop will wear a uniform, and a specialist will wear a white sterile garment. At a negligible look, these outfits mention to individuals what an individual accomplishes professionally.

Nonverbal communication assumes a significant job by the way we pass on importance and data to other people, just as how we decipher the activities of everyone around us. The significant thing to recollect when taking a gander at such nonverbal practices is to think about the activities in gatherings. What an individual really says alongside their expressions, appearance, and manner of speaking may reveal to you a lot about what that individual is truly attempting to state.

Tips For Improving Your Nonverbal Communication

Solid communication abilities can help you in both your own and expert life. While verbal and composed communication abilities are significant, investigate has shown that nonverbal practices make up an enormous level of our everyday relational communication.

How might you improve your nonverbal communication abilities? The accompanying tips can assist you with figuring out how to read the nonverbal signals of others and upgrade your own capacity to impart viably.

1. Focus on Nonverbal Signals

Individuals can convey data from numerous points of view, so focus on things like eye contact, gestures, posture, body developments, and manner of speaking. These signals can pass on significant data that isn't articulated.

By giving nearer consideration to others' implicit practices, you will improve your own capacity to convey nonverbally.

2. Search for Incongruent Behaviors

In the event that somebody's words don't coordinate their nonverbal practices, you should give cautious consideration. For instance, somebody may disclose to you they are happy while scowling and gazing at the ground.

Research has indicated that when words neglect to coordinate with nonverbal signals, individuals will in general disregard what has been said and center rather around implicit expressions of states of mind, considerations, and feelings. So when somebody says a certain something, however their body language appears to recommend something different, it tends to be valuable to give additional consideration to those unpretentious nonverbal signals.

3. Use Good Eye Contact

Great eye contact is another fundamental nonverbal communication ability. At the point when individuals neglect to look at others without flinching, it can appear as though they are dodging or attempting to conceal something. Then again, an excessive amount of eye contact can appear to be fierce or threatening.

While eye contact is a significant piece of communication, recall that great eye contact doesn't mean gazing steadily at someone. How might you tell what amount of eye contact is right?

Some communication specialists suggest interims of eye contact enduring four to five seconds. Powerful eye contact should feel normal and agreeable for both you and the individual you are talking with.

4. Pose Inquiries About Nonverbal Signals

On the other hand that you are confounded about someone else's nonverbal signals, don't be reluctant to pose inquiries. A smart thought is to rehash back your translation of what has been said and request explanation. A case of this may be, "So what you are stating is that..."

Once in a while just posing such inquiries can loan a lot of clearness to a circumstance. For instance, an individual may be radiating sure nonverbal signals since he has something different on his mind. By inquisitive further into his message and plan, you may show signs of improvement thought of what he is truly attempting to state.

5. Use Signals to Make Communication More Meaningful

Recollect that verbal and nonverbal communication cooperate to pass on a message. You can improve your expressed communication by utilizing body language that strengthens and bolsters what you are stating. This can be particularly valuable when making introductions or when addressing an enormous gathering of individuals.

For instance, if you will probably seem sure and arranged during an introduction, you will need to concentrate on imparting nonverbal signs that guarantee that others consider you to be confident and competent. Standing solidly in one spot, shoulder back, and your weight adjusted on the two feet is an extraordinary method to pause dramatically.

6. Take a gander at Signals as a Whole

Another significant piece of good nonverbal communication abilities includes having the option to adopt an increasingly all-encompassing strategy to what an individual is conveying.

A solitary motion can mean any number of things, or possibly nothing by any means.

The way to precisely reading nonverbal conduct is to search for gatherings of signals that fortify a typical point.

In the event that you place an excessive amount of accentuation on only one signal out of many, you may arrive at an off base decision about what an individual is attempting to state.

7. Think about the Context

At the point when you are speaking with others, generally consider the circumstance and the setting wherein the communication happens. A few circumstances require increasingly formal practices that may be deciphered contrastingly in some other setting.

Consider whether nonverbal practices are fitting for the specific circumstance. On the other hand that you are attempting to improve your own nonverbal communication, focus on approaches to make your signals coordinate the degree of convention required by the circumstance.

For instance, the body language and nonverbal communication you use at work are most likely totally different from the kind of signals you would send on an easygoing Friday night out with companions. Endeavor to coordinate your nonverbal signals to the circumstance to guarantee that you are passing on the message you truly need to send.

8. Be Aware That Signals Can be Misread

As per somewhere in the range of, a confident handshake shows a solid character while a feeble handshake is taken as an absence of backbone. This model outlines a significant point about the plausibility of misreading nonverbal signals. A limp handshake may really show something different completely, for example, joint inflammation.

Continuously make sure to search for gatherings of conduct. An individual's general disposition is unmistakably more telling than a solitary signal saw in disengagement.

9. Practice, Practice, Practice

A few people simply appear to have a talent for utilizing nonverbal communication successfully and accurately deciphering signals from others. These individuals are regularly depicted as having the option to "read individuals."

As a general rule, you can fabricate this aptitude by giving cautious consideration to nonverbal conduct and rehearsing various sorts of nonverbal communication with others. By seeing nonverbal conduct and rehearsing your own aptitudes, you can significantly improve your communication capacities.

Nonverbal communication abilities are fundamental and can make it simpler to pass on your point and to read what others are attempting to let you know. A few people appear to stop by these aptitudes normally, yet anybody can improve their nonverbal abilities with training.

Chapter 1: Facial Expressions

As indicated, facial expressions should be interpreted among the entire set of body language but in this chapter, we will detail how to read facial expressions. Wrinkles convey the intensity of emotions and the degree of originality of the emotion. In most cases, wrinkles convey hardship and suffering as well as extreme anger. Wrinkles indicate that one is always smiling, senile or nasty.

Facial expressions and emotions are related. Facial expressions can create an emotional experience. Smiling tends to induce more pleasant moods while frowning induces negative moods. In this manner, facial expressions produce emotion by creating various physical changes in the body. People often assume that smiling means indicates happiness, while frowning indicates sadness.

Emotions are caused by other factors beyond facial expressions. For instance, emotions are largely a function of the human system of beliefs and stored information. In other terms, you feel angry when you score less than average marks because the current system equates that to not being smart enough and the stored information reminds you that you risk repeating the test or not securing a plum employment position and this entire make you feel hopeless, upset and stressed. There is a possibility that if the belief system did not deem less than average as a failure and the stored information shows a positive outlook for a such a score that you will feel happy or excited by the score.

Additionally, twitching your mouth randomly, either way indicates that one is deliberately not listening or degrading the importance of the message. The facial gesture is realized by closing the lips and randomly twitching the mouth to either the right or left akin to swirling the mouth with mouthwash. The facial expression is also to indicate outright disdain to the speaker or the message. The facial expression is considered a rude way of expressing disgust with the speaker or the message and should be avoided at all cost.

Where one shuts their lips tightly then it indicates the individual is feeling angry but does not wish to show the anger. Shutting the lips tightly may also indicate that the person is feeling unease but struggling to concentrate at all costs. The source of the discomfort could be the immediate neighbors, the message, or the speaker. Through this gesture, the individual is indicating that he or she simply wants the speaker to conclude the speech because not all people are enjoying the message.

When one is angry or strongly disapproves of what the speaker is saying then the person will grin. A grin indicates that the person is feeling disgusted by what is being said. In movies or during live interviews you probably so the interviewee grin when an issue or a person that the person feels is disgusting is mentioned. Showing a grin indicates that one harbors a strong dislike for the message or the speaker. A person that is feeling uncomfortable due to sitting on a hard chair, a poorly ventilated room or sitting next to a hostile neighbor may also show a grin which is not necessarily related to the message.

If one is happy then one is likely to have a less tense face and a smile. Positive news and positive emotions are manifested as a smile or a less tense facial look. On the other hand if one is processing negative emotions then the face of the person is likely to be tensed up due to exerting pressure on the body muscles. A genuine smile like when one is happy is wide by average curve and is temporary. A prolonged smile that is very wide suggests that the individual is smirking at the message or the speaker. A prolonged smile may also suggest the individual is faking the emotion.

By the same measure, a frozen face may indicate intense fear. For instance, you have seen terrified faces when attending a health awareness forum on sexually transmitted diseases or some medical condition that terrified the audience. In this setting, the face of the audience will appear as if it has been paused. The eyes and the mouth may remain stationary as the speaker presents the scary aspects of the medical condition. It appears negative emotions may slow down the normal conscious and unconscious movement of the muscles of the face.

Overall, human beings can recognize six general emotions when presented with any variety of facial expressions. These include fear, happiness, sadness, surprise, and disgust. Due to the universality of facial expressions with regard to emotion, it can be concluded that they are innate rather than learned behaviors. Interestingly, blind individuals use facial expressions that are similar to the facial expressions displayed by people who are not blind.

Aside from the cultural similarities, differences in facial expression of emotion happen across cultures. One, people are likely to correctly interpret the facial expression of people from their culture compared to those of other cultures. Nevertheless, most people are able to identify emotions from the facial expressions of others regardless of culture. The appropriateness of facial expressions varies among subcultures of the same cultural group. Compared to the Japanese, Americans readily manifest anger and this shows that individuals express emotion differentially across cultures.

If you are a teacher or trainer then you encounter facial expressions from your students frequently. Assuming that you are a teacher then you have noticed facial expressions indicating shock, uneasiness, and disapproval when you announce tests or indicate that the scores are out. Form these facial expressions you will concur that the students feel uncomfortable, uncertain and worried. The students will show lines of wrinkles, look down, eyes wide open and mouths agape when sudden and uncomfortable news is announced. Even though the students may indicate that they are prepared for the test, their facial expressions suggest otherwise.

Like all forms of communication, effective reading of facial expressions will happen where the target person is unaware that you are reading even though they understand that their facial expressions are integral to the overall communication. In other terms, when one becomes aware that he or she is being studied than the person will act in an expected manner or simply freeze expected reaction. It is akin to realizing that someone is feeling you.

Since the underlying emotion affects the facial expression that one shows. As indicated the body language overrides verbal communication which helps reveal the true status of an individual. One possible argument of the body language triumphing over verbal communication could be because the body prioritizes its physiological needs over other needs. The physiological needs are critical to the survivability of an individual. Over centuries the human body could have been programmed to increase survivability rate by prioritizing physiological needs. Body language largely indicates the physiological state of an individual which is meant to help the individual and others respect the true physiological status of the person.

Imagine what could happen where one is sickly and it is worsening but the person manages to manifest convincing body language of happiness and enthusiasm. The outcome would be prioritizing the emotional needs of the individual over the physiological needs. Apart from laboratory tests and physical examination, it would be difficult for other people to realize that something is amiss and ask the individual to take rest. Without illness, when one feels anxious about the audience then he or she manifests disharmony of the physiological status and there is a necessity to make the person and the audience aware that the individual is suffering and that they should be understanding of the individual.

Chapter 2: Micro Expressions

Micro expression is the involuntary natural reaction we give after we receive a stimulus that triggers an emotional reaction. It's an involuntary facial expression that we show during an experience, it's quick and instance. While the regular facial expression is usually prolonged and easy to fake. The face and eyes are the windows to the soul if you know how to read expressions you can better understand how a person really feels or what they are thinking.

There are 7 universal micro expressions, which include contempt, surprise, happiness, sadness, fear, anger, and disgust. Micro expressions often occur as fast as 1/15 to 1/25 of a second, which are milliseconds, so these are very hard to catch. Facial expressions are a reflection of a person's true feeling it indicates the real emotions of people. Dr. Paul Ekman discovered that facial expressions are universal all over the world. People in Europe have the same expression has people in North America, Asia, and Africa. Dr.Ekman also discovered that people who are blind from birth also have the same facial expressions.

Micro expression helps to conceal true emotions, it helps to hide expressions during a job interview, it helps to hide our nervousness and that we may have inefficiency in our skills and abilities. Micro expressions will give away our true emotions and feelings. Typically only people that are knowledgeable in this area can detect micro expressions, "if" they are looking out to catch them because they are quick and instantaneous for a millisecond. Micro expression is so hard to notice that when researchers try to catch them they have to use highspeed cameras.

If we can understand how to detect micro expressions, this can boost your social skills as you will now have the ability to detect emotional expressions from other people. If you are around someone and you are trying to impress them and you see a negative micro expression that can be an indication that they are not interested in you, or they may not be comfortable with a topic you are discussing.

Here is how microexpressions look for negative emotions:

- Puckering lips, squinting - This signal dislike, disinterest, and disengagement.

- Disappearing lips - this signal stress and pressure

- Eyelid fluttering - this signal discomfort, that the person could
be uncomfortable

- Closed lip or tighten lip smile - indicate that someone does not wish to speak or engage in a conversation

- Sneer- this indicates disrespect, contempt, and dislike.

- The upturn of inner eyebrows - indicates that the person is feeling sadness

Ekman has identified seven expressions that are used among people from all walks of life. If we can understand them and read them efficiently we can see people's true emotions. Let's have a look at the seven universal microexpressions:

Anger

You can see anger microexpression in the upper part of the face, the eyebrows become raised and curved, the skin below the brow is stretch, your forehead become wrinkles, your eyelid becomes open the white of the eyes start showing the top and the bottom, jaws dropped and the teeth are parted. When you are angry vertical lines will appear between your eyebrows, your eyes are in hard stare and your nostrils will seem dilated.

Fear

This expression you will see the person showing tension on their brows that's drawn together and their eyes will be wide open, allowing us to have a clearer vision to see the coming danger. In the lower part of the face, the jaw will be loose, which allows us to yell or cry for help. The upper eyelid will be raised, the upper white of the eyes will show but not the lower. When you see these facial expressions you can tell that a person is fearful.

Surprise

When you observe this facial expression, you will see raise eyebrows, with widened eyes. In the lower part of the face, the jaw will be loose and mouth open. The skin below the brow will be stretch and you will see long horizontal wrinkles across the forehead. You will see the white of the eyes both below and above. The jaws will drop and teeth are parted but there will be no visible tension in the mouth.

SADNESS

This microexpression is one of the easiest to identify and the hardest to fake. You will see changes in the eyebrow they will subtly meet each other in the center, the mouth is arched downwards. The skin below the eyebrows will form a triangle, the jaws will come up and the lips will pout out.

DISDAIN

With this facial expression, you will see the upper part of the face shapes changes, one part of the mouth will be raised and the other will form a partial smile. The upper lip may be exposed with the cheeks raised and the nose will show wrinkles.

Disgust

This expression we will see the entire facial expression is concentrated in the mouth and nose.

The nose will wrinkle and the upper part of the lip is raised, showing the upper teeth

Happiness

Happiness is expressed through squinted eyes and wrinkles on the side of the face and the bottom eyelids. The corners of the lips will be drawn back and up, teeth will be exposed even though the mouth won't necessarily be parted. The person's cheeks will be raised and there will be wrinkles at the corner of the eyes.

Chapter 3: The Voice

There are four indicators of the quality of one's voice. They are one's intonation, volume, pitch, and rate of speech. If the voice is monotone and rather flat, they are probably bored or boring. The lack of animation in the voice could also indicate the speaker is tired. If the person's voice sounds clear and concise, they most usually are confident and powerful, more like the Leader Personality Type. If the volume is quiet or soft, the person is thought to be shy, or it could even mean they have a secret they don't want to share.

The rate of speech is also quite important when analyzing others, especially if you are attempting to mirror them to increase the chances of connectivity. For example, Leader Personality Types will usually speak fast and loud, and you need to match their volume and rate. Identifiers often speak slower than Leaders, and their pitch is more soothing than the dominant personality type. The voice can be a strong descriptive element of the individual's personality type.

By now, you have probably caught on that every movement has a message. Verify the meaning of some of the nonverbal languages by other things, such as one's words, voice, facial expressions, and gestures. To discover one's real message, you must become a student of human behavior, studying the other's movements, speech pattern, attitude, words, gestures, and expressions to analyze people successfully.

You've been introduced to the nonverbal language and the four main personality types, and to how you form accurate perceptions, but all these things are not separate from one another. They all blend to create effective communications. In the next chapter, you'll be asked to read some scenarios and identify the personality types, nonverbal indicators, and interpret the intended message.

Chapter 4: Decoding the Eyes

When children are being evaluated for neurological challenges, one of the main observable points is their ability to maintain good eye contact. Although an intricate detail, the ability to lock eyes with someone else during conversation speaks wonders to the child's level of function. If a child is able to maintain direct eye contact throughout the course of their assessments, they are deemed high on the social spectrum. However, the inability to maintain eye contact could be a sign of autism or even social anxiety. The eyes reveal small truths to the inner workings of our biology.

Typically, what is the first thing you look at when meeting someone? Usually, their eyes reveal aspects of beauty that are attractive to first encounters. Many even remember people because of the shape, color, and size of the eyes. We are neurotically programmed to be visual creatures who make associations through what we see. Generally, these associations are labeled by what we give off. Since every aspect of the body works in conjunction with the brain, how do our eyes communicate with certain receptors?

The Eye Meets the Brain

The retina is like the gatekeeper of the eye. Everything we see, through the exchange of light, passes through the retina and is then transferred to two different aspects of the eye: rods which manage our ability to see at night, and cones which handle our daily vision activities such as color translation, reading, writing, and scanning. Various neurons travel throughout the eye and communicate with different functions within the eye to carry unique signals. These signals are then carried through the optic nerve into the cerebral cortex. The cerebral cortex is like the movie theatre of the brain. It controls our visual receptors that are responsible for perception, memory, and thoughts. When our eye sees something pleasurable, researchers have discovered that the pupil actually expands. This phenomenon proves that what we see is how we think. Through this, we can formulate opinions, draw conclusions, and even interpret body movements.

There are certain concrete directions carried out by the eyes that indicate true intentions:

Right glance: This is used to remember something, maybe a name, face, song, or book.

Left glance: This is used to remember physical features such as color, shape, texture, and other visual stimulants.

Glancing downward in a right position: This controls our imagination and what we believe something to be like.

Glancing downward towards the left: Inner communication, the conversations we have with the self.

The way our eyes work with the brain and perception is key to understanding body language. Since we use every aspect of our body to communicate, it is only natural that the eyes play a major role in this form of communication. Sure, the eyes may seem one dimensional to the untrained individual. However, their slight movements can indicate everything you need to know about a person. Let's consider a few examples.

<u>Direct</u> Eye Contact

Direct eye contact can mean a caveat of emotions. Surely, self-confidence is one of the primary indicators of locking eyes. When vetting for a job, recruiters will often instruct their interviewees to look the interviewer in the eye in order to display awareness. This shows the interviewer that you aren't intimidated and can take on any task. Similarly, animals utilize eye contact when interpreting dominance. For example, a trainer will often look a dog in the eye that he is training in order to establish dominance. By the trainer locking eyes and refusing to move, the dog will know to listen to his commands. Humans also communicate via dominant signals. Direct eye contact trumps fear.

It shows that you are comfortable with the conversation, and it even indicates interest.

In addition, balance is the key to everything. Too much direct eye contact could prove to be intimidating to the receiving individual. This intense stare could cause others to feel uncomfortable, with them maybe even questioning your overall sanity. Imagine engaging in a conversation with someone who never stopped looking into your eyes. Even when you looked away, their eyes were still locked on yours. Surely, you would chalk them up to be extremely strange. It's always important to be cognizant of what your eyes are doing as staring, in some cultures, could be viewed as rude.

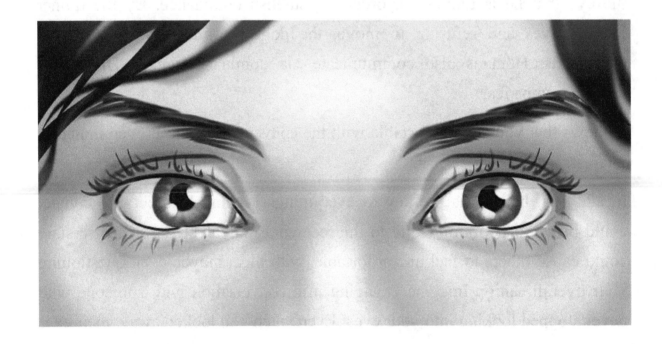

Looking Away

When a person avoids eye contact, this is typically a sign of low selfconfidence. The person may be uncomfortable with the conversation, person, or environment they are in. In addition, anxiety surrounding social settings can make a person apprehensive to locking eyes with someone they don't know.

Avoiding eye contact also signals inner conflict. Perhaps they are fighting against subconscious urges of attraction; therefore, they avoid making eye contact; or maybe they are hiding something that heightens their anxiety. This doesn't indicate that a person is devious or even untrustworthy. They may suffer from debilitating self-consciousness that overwhelms their disposition.

Dilated Pupils

The pupils generate intricate signals that identify even the smallest of changes within the body. Studies have shown that when people are presented with a challenging question, their pupils grow larger. When the brain is forced to think beyond its capabilities, the pupils actually become narrow, according to a 1973 study. The pupils are also key indicators of stress on the brain. Health care professionals will shine a small flashlight into the eyes of their patients in order to check the normality of their pupils. If the pupils are balanced in size and react to the shining light, the brain isn't experiencing distress. However, any imbalance could indicate a serious brain injury.

As mentioned earlier, dilated pupils express extreme interest, even agreement. When you see or hear something that sparks your attention, your pupils will dilate almost immediately. The same occurs when a person is shown a representation of something they agree with. In 1969, a revered researcher sought to prove the notion that the pupils' dilation can reveal political affiliations. By showing participants pictures of political figures they admired, the participants' eyes dilated. However, when shown an opposing photo, the pupils grew narrow; often snake-like.

What Our Visual Directions Indicate

The positioning of our eyes and what we choose to focus on during a conversation can speak volumes. For instance, glancing downward could indicate shame, even submission. When children are being reprimanded, they are often looking down to show their personal disdain for their behavior. In ancient Chinese culture, one typically looked down in a submissive form to show respect to those in authority. On the contrary, glaring upward indicated traits of haughtiness. It is often associated with being bored or not wanting to engage in the activity at hand. In addition, looking up signals uncertainty. Movies and television shows may depict a teenager taking a test and looking up because they are unaware of the answer.

Sideways glances are often cues for internal irritation. For example, when a coworker you dislike walks into the room, you may inadvertently look at them sideways, simply because they are the bane of your existence. This can also occur when engaging with individuals who annoy you. The takeaway from the sideways stare is discontentment. When you see something that just isn't right, or even a sneaky individual, you may give them the side-eye. This demonstrates total repulsion for their attitude, reputation, or even their expressions.

Many would attribute squinting to being unable to see. While true, a squint can also mimic signs of disbelief or confusion. One may hear something and want more information. Thus, they squint their eyes while listening; it's almost as if they are saying, "I don't believe you…I need more answers!"

Stress can induce quick blinking which causes a person to go into a frenzy. You may notice a person rapidly blinking while moving frantically to finish a task. This could be accompanied by sweat or trembling. On the contrary, excessive blinking could be a subtle sign of arrogance. A boss, for example, may blink rapidly while speaking to an employee in an attempt to dismiss their conversation. This fast-action blinking essentially blinds the boss from the employee for less than a second, indicating that they would rather be engaging in something else.

A direct gaze paired with a lowered lid and head indicates extreme attraction. It's almost likened to a "come hither" invitation between mates. This gaze is heightened through sexual attraction and may even induce pupil dilation.

Inability to Focus and Attention Deficit

An eye nystagmus identifies how long it takes the body to focus on one point after undergoing extreme movement. If a person has a nystagmus lasting longer than 14 seconds, they may have challenges with keeping focused. One academic facility tests the accuracy of a child's nystagmus by spinning them a number of times and having them glance up towards the ceiling. The eyes then move rapidly, sometimes dilating, then narrowing. The longer it takes the child to stabilize is documented. They further engage in this spinning activity weekly with the hopes of strengthening their ability to remain focused on one thing despite many distractions. As they continue to grow a tolerance, their eyes will stabilize in a lower amount of time. The goal is to strengthen their ability to dismiss outward distractions which will help with attention deficit disorder. The movement of the eyes tell trained professionals exactly how much assistance a child will need and in what specific area. Aren't the eyes magnificent?

Our eyes open the door to many revelations of the self. You are able to gain psychological perspective on how you perceive yourself and others by a simple glance! Irritation, lust, attraction, and even doubt can be detected by paying close attention. Since the eyes have a direct pathway to the brain, it is only natural that they are the gatekeepers of the soul. By implementing these quick tips into your social life, you will have the grand ability to analyze a person in a complex manner. Of course, the eyes are also home to detecting deceit. As we continue to travel through our body language adventure, we will soon learn how the eyes can reveal the trustworthiness of an individual.

Chapter 5: The Meaning of Body Posture

The way you sit & stand when interacting with others can communicate a great deal about you to them without you or them being conscious about it. If you somehow find that statement a bit vague, consider this: have you ever felt "suspicious" of someone who looks nice, talks nice, & smells nice? I mean despite the "nice" appearance, have you ever felt that deep inside, this actually may be a dubious character that's just trying to put one over you? If you have, then you may not have been aware of it, but you were actually able to pick up on his or her body language - particularly their body positions - on a subconscious level. Through their posture, you were also able to somehow pick up on what they're really about on a subconscious level. & if you can master the art of using body language to your advantage, you can very easily make people trust you & be persuaded by you. Eventually, you can also succeed in your relationships & in your career or business life.

Let's take a look at some of the most common positions that contribute to your body language.

Sitting positions

A lot of people - maybe you included - aren't aware but the way we sit can tell others much about how we're feeling at the moment or even our current mood, as well as our personality. The way we sit can actually project a shy or insecure vibe or project a more confident, even aggressive one. Let's take a look at these sitting positions.

The Cross-Legged Position

For the most part, sitting with legs crossed projects a feeling of being carefree
& open. Crossing the legs with knees spread to the side can actually give people the subconscious impression that physically, you're all game to take on new ideas, which can also be subconsciously perceived to mean that emotionally speaking, you're also open to some new things. Being open means you're a person that's fun & interesting to be with, which can actually make more people be drawn to you naturally.

The Erect Sitting Position

Without thinking much about it, it's also easy to see that a person who usually sits this way is a confident, reliable, & secure one. & if you sit this way most of the time, regardless if consciously or unconsciously, people will think of you as such a person. & this's a great thing to have, especially when it comes to doing business with others. This's because if people think you're actually reliable & secure, they'll more easily trust you to do business with you. & don't get me started about how this can help you in your dating or love life.

The Reclined Sitting Position

Of all the sitting positions, this one's perhaps the one that can give you a Big Bang Theory vibe, i.e., an analytical one. Leaning back is a gesture that simply shows you're able to properly think about or observe situations without necessarily or hastily acting upon them. This also means you may be more objective than most other people being able to separate yourself enough from a situation to think about it first before taking action. & from a relational perspective, this can give others the impression that you're a person who's very much aware of how others feel, which can also help you connect to people on a deeper level & easily earn their trust & loyalty.

Crossed Ankle Sitting Position

In most cases, sitting with ankles crossed simply gives others the impression that the person sitting in this position isn't only elegant & refined but is also humble & open-minded. Coupled with slightly open legs, this position conveys a feeling of being comfortable both under one's own skin & in the environment.

Clutching Armrests Sitting Position

Sitting stiffly & are practically clutching at the chair's armrests shows awareness of & sensitivity to one's surroundings. & by clutching on armrests, the seated person comes across to most other people as emotionally & physically unsure because of the need to clutch on to the chair's armrests for stability most of the time.

But merely using the armrests by resting your arms on them instead of actually clutching to them can also give a much different impression - an opposite one in fact. Doing so can communicate that you're a stable person – emotionally, physically, & mentally - so much so that people are predisposed to depending on you for their own emotional & intellectual stability. You'll likely become their figurative armrests.

Crossed Arm Sitting Position

Often times crossed arms are often perceived as indicators of confidence, defensiveness, & strength. But it can also be taken as an indicator of being closed to new ideas or being protective of one's self, with arms crossed in front of the body being taken to mean as protection of one's body from the rest of the world. Either way, a crossed arm sitting position is actually a body language that says a person is neither open nor weak.

Sidesaddle Sitting Position

If you're a lady, then this one's for you specifically. The amazing sidesaddle sitting position is one where you sit with your knees to the side. This type of sitting position basically communicates a naturally sweet, caring, & delicate personality. & oh...it can also communicate a personality that's a wee bit flirtatious. So choose wisely to whom you'll show this particular body position. & when you point your knees & chest to the other person, it can be subconsciously taken as being available & open to something new, i.e., a possible relationship.

Hands on Lap Sitting Position

When your hands are on your thighs & are still, it can be construed as a sign that you're a thoughtful & shy person. Also, you can come across as a calm & collected person if you're actually able to keep your hands still while sitting down.

Dead Center Sitting Position

Sitting smack in the center of a couch, bench, or even table communicates to others that you're a totally confident person. Why? It's because people who aren't confident, i.e., insecure or even tentative, tend to worry about where to sit down - they practically fuss over where they should sit & sitting in the center is very uncomfortable for most of them. So by sitting in the middle, it essentially communicates to others that you're not afraid of being in the center of attention & that you can choose to sit anywhere you want to. & by subtly communicating to others that you're confident, you can also come across & friendly & bold, which can make it easier for you to establish rapport with others, which's a crucial skill for business.

Legs on Chair Arm Sitting Position

This's a sitting position that's mostly taken by men as it also makes use of the spread legs position. This sitting position is also one where a person stakes his ownership of the chair & communicates an aggressive & informal attitude.

While it's not unusual to see this sitting position among two friends who're whiling time away joking & laughing with each other, it's not appropriate for other, more serious situations. For example, you're a boss & your subordinate comes to you after making a big mistake at work, which's totally ok with you. Say your subordinate felt really bad about the mistake & he sits in front of your table with head held low & hands on his knees - a submissive body language. Let's say after listening for a while to what your subordinate has to say, you quickly adopt a legs on chair arm position. By doing so, you've just subtly communicated to your subordinate that you don't give a rat's ass about how he's feeling & that he's wasting your time. It's as if you're telling him you're tired of the same old story. Through this position, you're actually coming off as aggressively dismissing your subordinate's feelings.

Now maybe the reason you're dismissing your subordinate's feelings is actually a very good one: that you don't think he's done anything seriously wrong & that he shouldn't feel that bad about his mistake. Now even if you verbally communicate that, remember how powerful body language can be when it comes to communicating with others - about how it's more powerful than verbal communications? Therefore, even if you meant well & really wanted to encourage him, your body language, i.e., the legs-on-the-chair-arm position, essentially communicates a vastly different message; one that aggressively says you're not interested in how he feels & that he's just wasting your time.

On your end, you should actually avoid this body language at all costs, save for informal interactions with people who you already have deep relationships with. Now if you use this in a business setting, chances are high that you'll perhaps just piss off your counterparties & substantially lower your chances of being able to successfully discuss or negotiate with them & persuade them to side with you.

If during a business or even professional meeting, the other person takes this stance, it's a sign that this person thinks lowly of you & believes he can get away with everything with you. That's unless you respond accordingly. How can you do so without actually coming across as angry or disruptive?

You can make a light & funny but indirect attempt to tell him that you noticed he's doing that posture & that it's not appropriate. For example, you can perhaps half-jokingly tell him that his pants have split between his legs or even putting something just in front of him at a distance that'd require him to break the position & ask him to look at that thing. If he returns to the position, just continue breaking it in a subtle & if possible, a funny way.

The Chair Straddling Sitting Position

Ages ago, it normally used to be that men used shields for protection against their enemies' weapons. These days, people whatever's available to symbolize their attempts at protecting themselves against the perceived verbal & physical attacks. & these attempts may include hiding behind an object - such as doors, fences, or even gates, & by straddling a chair.

By straddling a chair, a person is also able to symbolically protect him or herself using a chair's backside. Moreover, such a position can make a person look dominant & aggressive, which can help fend off "attackers." & because straddling a chair requires a spread legs posture, it also allows a person to take up more space & thus, adding extra assertion to the posture.

When you encounter a straddler, chances are that he or she's a person with a very domineering personality who likes controlling others as soon as they become bored with their interactions. & in most cases, they're very discreet, i.e., you hardly notice them slipping into this sitting position during interaction. So how do you handle such a person, take the power back, & increase your chances of successfully persuading him or her to your way position?

As with other dominating positions, change your position so that they'll also be forced to break theirs. For example, you can stand up & go behind him or her, which will force her to turn around & break the straddling position in order to continue interacting with you. The chances of this working are also high because by going behind the straddler, you put him or her in a position where he or she just can't cover his or her back, which's a vulnerable position that people with strong personalities don't like.

Now, what if the straddler is sitting on swivel chair that can also very easily turn around without having to break the straddling position? Breaking his or her perceived dominance will actually require you to add another action to changing your position: moving into his or her personal space. After standing up to continue conversing with a straddler, which also puts you in a position to look down on him or her, moving in to his or her personal space will also make it very uncomfortable for him or her to continue straddling the chair, which will eventually force him or her to finally abandon the straddling position & change into something more comfortable.

Standing positions

When standing up, the legs & feet are obviously the body parts that do most of the work. & because of this, legs & feet can be a very good source of information - whether about you or others. But how's this so?

Dr. Paul Ekman & William Friesen have conducted researches on deceptive habits & those researches have shown that people who're lying tend to give away more signals of such through lower body movements, regardless of gender. It appears that the reason for this's consciousness of movements - or lack thereof. People, in general, are more aware of their upper body movements & gestures & aren't as conscious of lower body part ones. This's probably because the legs & feet are generally out of the lines of sight of people when interacting with others & so most people aren't able to consciously control their lower body movements compared to upper body ones.

Being aware of the common standing positions & the subconscious messages they generally send can help you effectively communicate to others & to read them with relatively high accuracy.

The Parallel Stance Standing Position

This standing position is one taken usually by a subordinate & is taken by standing with both legs straight & both feet positioned closely with each other. This's a formal standing position that can subconsciously communicate a neutral attitude such as that of a child student when talking to the teacher, an army member when addressing his commanding officer, or standing in front of a panel of judges while simply waiting for their verdict during a competition.

This particular standing position is also relatively more precarious than the others because feet close together while actually standing is a relatively weak standing foundation compared to wider-stance ones. With this position, you can be easily pushed out of balance when caught off guard or you can also do the same to another person.

As mentioned earlier, this's a stand taken by people who're usually neutral on a particular topic or situation, i.e., they're unsure, tentative, or hesitant.

The Spread Legs Standing Position

With this standing position, which's normally a position taken by men, subconsciously or subtly communicates a stable, resolute, & unmoving posture. By taking this position, you can subtly communicate to other people that you'll stand your ground & you're showing your dominance. This standing position is taken with legs straight but this time, both feet are actually positioned widely apart - normally wider than shoulder width - & bodyweight equally distributed between both feet.

One of the main reasons why this's a predominantly male standing position is average height, i.e., men are generally taller than women & thus, have higher centers of gravity. But height notwithstanding, it's also used more by men because it actually uses the genital area to highlight dominance through a virile look, which isn't the case with ladies. Another reason is that men normally just don't wear skirts, which can make the spread legs standing position a bit challenging & uncomfortable.

And more than just convincing others to look at you with a positive view, adapting the spread legs standing position can also easily help you feel much better about yourself during times when you're feeling down. Couple this standing position with your shoulders pulled back & head held high, it's a short matter of time before your motion or position will affect your emotion, i.e., you'll feel more confident & positive about yourself.

Foot Forward Standing Position

This position, done by with one leg & foot forward, can help you send subconscious signals to other people about the direction you want to go or the person in a group you find most interesting or even attractive. In particular, the direction or person your lead foot is pointing to is a subtle way of simply telling others where you want to go or who the most interesting person in the group for you is, respectively.

Crossed Legs Standing Position

When in a gathering, I want you to do something: observe the people around you who're standing & watch out for those who're doing so with crossed arms & legs. In particular, I'd like you to observe how far they're from other people compared to those whose legs & arms aren't crossed. You'll find that they position themselves farther to others than those whose legs & arms are open while standing. Closed legs communicate that a person has a generally closed or defensive attitude, which's symbolized by crossed legs that appear to deny access to the genital area.

There's a good chance that crossed legs & arms while standing up merely communicate that the person is feeling cold & not defensive. So how'd you know? First, observe the temperature of the place. If it's cold, it's also probably done as a way to keep warm. Yet another way is to check where the hands are placed. If they're tucked between armpits, they're cold. If the legs are straight, pressed hard against each other, & stiff, chances are it's an attempt to keep warm rather than a defensive attitude.

Chapter 6: Body Language & Emotions

Emotions have purposes – they motivate us, help us form quick decisions, give us feedback, & help us relate to other people. Our bodies, especially our faces, also naturally reveal our emotions because they guide how others will relate to us. Before humans have invented spoken language, they've relied on visual signals & communicated through actions. This has also become embedded in our biology, so what we feel inside gets translated through our behavior, & we can easily tell what others feel by watching how they behave.

If you observe closely, you may be able to tell what a person is really feeling even if there're no obvious indicators such as laughs or tears. However, remember that the following indicators may not always mean that a person is actually feeling the specified emotion. You must also consider the situation as well as what the person is talking about.

There're the basic emotions:

Love – Love is a pleasant emotion that keeps people together. It's manifested by attentiveness, caring gestures, & signs of arousal.

Anger – this's felt when a person thinks that he or she's being violated in a way, or when he/she can't meet a goal. Anger simply gives a boost of energy that aims to help the person attain his/her goal & fight off enemies. Anger leads to aggressive body language.

Happiness – A person feels joy when he/she achieves goals & has his/her needs met. This's the brain's reward for good things done, & this pleasant emotion encourages more of the same actions that have created joy. Also happiness result to a relaxed & open body language.

Fear – Fear causes an individual to avoid harm. It also occurs when a person's wellbeing is threatened, or if there's a possibility that he or she won't have his/her needs met. Defensive body language is a result of this emotion.

Surprise - Surprise occurs to quickly boost a person's attention & make him/her remember an unexpected incident. This will quickly make him/her be more prepared for it when it happens again. Being surprised suddenly causes a person to open his/her eyes wide to gather more visual information, open his/her mouth & scream to alert other people, & to leap backwards to avoid possible danger.

Sadness – Sadness accompanies the loss of something valuable. It simply motivates a person to protect the people & things that're dear to him/her. A sad person has a decreased energy & moves more slowly. This's because energy is directed towards ruminating over the loss & diverted away from physical activity.

Other emotions are variations of these primary ones:

- Affection, longing, & lust are forms love.

- Disgust, frustration, irritation, envy, & rage are related to anger.

- Pride, optimism, contentment, cheerfulness, & relief are some manifestations of happiness.

- Fear can also express itself in anxiety & horror.

- Sadness can be felt as agony, disappointment, displeasure, shame, pity, & humiliation.

These're some body language clusters that're associated with emotions:

Desire: pupils dilated, eyes wide, blushing, head & body inclined towards the desired person or thing, lips smiling or even slightly apart

Pleasure: eyes closed (to concentrate on the sensation) or even wide (to see more), slow movements, outstretched limbs, arched back, head tilted backwards, rapid breathing

Affection: hugs, gentle touches, nearness, kisses, protective gestures (such as shielding the other person from an aggressor)

Friendliness: staying close but also respecting personal space, smiling, open body language, making playful gestures such as winks & high-fives

Flirtatiousness: hair flipping, self-grooming, winking, catching the other person's gaze, touching, prolonged eye contact, posing like a cowboy (hands gripping the belt, or with hands at the hips & fingers pointing to the crotch), protruding breasts (for a woman), playing with a cylindrical object, straightening the back, lowered head while looking (for women)

Anger: eyebrows pulled down towards the center, wide eyes gazing intently, wrinkled forehead, chin or head jutting out, jaw clenched, lips pressed together, teeth bared, snarling sounds, flaring nostrils (this allows more air to enter the lungs during a fight), stomping feet, leaning forward, invading the other person's personal space, flailing arms, hands curled into fists

Annoyance (a mild form of anger): narrowed eyes, rolling eyes, lips pressed together, sighing

Frustration: running hands through the hair, shaking head, white knuckles

Envy: staring, chin pushed out, nose wrinkled, tightly pressed lips or mouth corners falling, crossed arms

Jealousy: It is same as the above but with a possessive body language (such as wrapping an arm around the person's mate or even pulling him/her away from the offender)

Disgust: head & eyes turning away, wrinkled nose, sneering, flared nostrils, closed mouth, lifted upper lip, tongue showing, chin held forward

Possessiveness: Simply putting hands on the person or even object, standing in someone's space, or facing the person directly, warding off other people who may get near, or even gripping handshake

Reluctance: putting hands over the ears, closed body language, dragging movements, nose pinching, turning head away, looking down or even sideways, folded arms

Relief: smiling or even mouth tilted down, lowered head, the inner corners of the eyebrows raised with the other edges lowered, sighing

Happiness: laughing, smiling mouth, raised cheeks, wrinkled eye corners, eyebrows raised slightly

Excitement: rapidly rubbing hands together (not slowly – if the person is perhaps rubbing his hands slowly, it basically means that he/ she's taking advantage of someone else), wide grin, screaming, jumping, laughing, energetic handshakes

Amusement: slapping thighs, laughing, clapping hands, stomping the feet

Victorious: chin up, fist/s punching the air, screaming joyously

Fear: wide eyes, raised eyebrows, mouth open or with the corners drooping, averting eye contact (to prevent aggravating someone), head down & chin tucked in (to protect the body), hunched shoulders, pale face & limbs, sweating, dry mouth & throat (the person may lick his/her lips, drink a glass of water, swallow frequently, or rub the throat), shaky voice, jerky motions (signs of wanting to run away), tensed muscles, arms and/or legs wrapped around objects (to gain support), cowering, shaking

Anxiety: shaking lower lip, wrinkled chin, eyebrows pushed together, head tilted downwards, rapid breathing, fidgeting (a sign of pent-up energy), eyes darting from side to side (to spot danger),

Surprise/shock: eyes opened wide, mouth gaping, eyebrows lifted, lowered chin, leaping backwards, head pushed back or tilted to one side, sudden movements, one hand covers the mouth, slapping head

Overwhelmed: palms pressed against forehead, eyes wide open, leaning against a wall, grasping the chair or even table for support, covering eyes

Awe (a mixture of interest, surprise, & fear): mouth agape, staring, stepping backwards, rigid body

Sadness: eyes downcast, crying or wet eyes, head down, eyebrows brought together & raised to the center of the forehead, lips quivering or downturned, drooping gestures, slouched body, monotonous voice

Pity: damp eyes, eyebrows pushed together, prolonged eye contact, mouth drooping at the corners, head tilted to one side

Humiliation: lowered eyebrows, blushing, head & eyes lowered, averting gaze, fake smile (to appease others), covering face

Interest: maintained eye contact, head and/or body leaning towards the object of interest, narrowed eyes (focusing on the person or object), lips smiling or pressed together lightly, slow nodding, leaning forward to the speaker or even towards the object/person that's interesting

Boredom: averting gaze, lips pushed back to one side, expressionless face, rigid body, head supported with one hand, with eyes possibly looking out through the fingers, fidgeting (this reveals a barely controlled urge to go somewhere else), looking far away (viewing or imagining something else that's more interesting), performing repetitious actions, fidgeting, slouching, leaning against the chair or wall

Impatience: quick nodding, fidgeting, sighing, checking his/her watch

Thinking: resting the chin on one hand, rubbing chin, squinting eyes, lips shut, eyebrows pulled together

Suspicious: narrowed eyes, shaking head, raising one eyebrow, closed body language, false smile

Fatigue: rubbing eyes, yawning, slouching, staring blankly, sighing, lowered head, crossed arms, clenched teeth, leaning back, doing stretches, propping head up with a hand

Chapter 7: The Silence Of A Thousand Words

You may find this surprising to hear at first, but we make major & serious life decisions based on the judgements we derive from body language. I know this sounds extreme at the beginning, but listen to these examples:

I could quote a lot of names & studies right now, but I want to keep this personal at the beginning. I'll follow up with all of the research studies later on, but from your own life, I can easily show you how you use your judgements on body language to shape your actions.

You've seen interviews take place at your job. You may even be in charge to conducting those interviews. You've probably noticed then that the people who're hired are the ones that make the proper social cues. They make eye contact, they shake your hand with a firm handshake. They don't fidget, even look around the room, or stutter.

All in all, they appear confident & competent, so they get the job.

But that's just one example. Consider your love life. If you see a man or a woman that you're attracted to, & you hope to get the attention of, you'll automatically do things to get that attention. Perhaps you do the clichés of laughing loudly or talking loudly. Perhaps you do things to show off.

If you see that they're interested, it only adds fuel to the fire, but if you see that they don't care, that they've a ring on their finger, or that they just don't have an interest in you, the act stops.

You base what you do, based on what the other person does.

This's a truth that branches out even further than our social lives

In courtrooms, people who're under fire for one reason or another can hope to get a better outcome based on if the judge & jury like them. This's subliminal & often subconscious, but if their facial expressions, their eye contact, & their body cues in general impress those around them, they're given a lesser sentence, or perhaps set free all together.

Politicians are also part of this realm. In a Princeton study, it was actually shown that what we perceive in the facial expression of a politician in just a single second or two has over 70% influence on how we vote.

Why?

Because we actually put a lot of trust into our own perception of things. Not how things really are, but what we think they are in reality.

Have you ever met someone, & found you'd a mutual acquaintance? Perhaps this mutual acquaintance is someone you don't know well, but perhaps your new friend knows quite well. They start telling you all kinds of things you never knew about your mutual acquaintance, & you come to realize this's because you haven't ever asked.

You see this person, perhaps even daily, but you never actually talk to them. Maybe it was the look on their face, which somehow made you consider them to be unfriendly without even speaking. Perhaps it was the way they held their arms at their side, or perhaps the way they sat at lunch. It may've even been a combination of any of these things, but you suddenly realize you formed opinions on this person without ever speaking to them.

We do it this to people we meet on the street, we do it to people we're putting into positions of power over us, & we do it to each other every single day.

Consider this example:

You see one of your coworkers at work, someone that you typically see bright & cheery, but today they aren't smiling. Today, they just keep their eyes on their work, don't move around much, & just have an all-around attitude of trying to keep to themselves.

From this, you derive that they must perhaps be in a bad mood. You don't know why, you don't ask why, you may perhaps not even care why, but you stay away from them & go about your own day, simply because of what you assume them to be feeling.

A perfect example of this's the trend in society to label certain people as having a "resting angry face".

If you've ever spent any time on social media, you know what this is. You may even be a person that has one. Someone that looks like they're unfriendly because of how their face is shaped.

They go through life, & are treated as though they aren't a very nice person, because of how their face looks in its normal countenance. There's countless jokes & clips made out of this idea, but if you analyze the reason behind this joke, you'll see that I'm right.

We all form opinions & judgements on people based on nothing more than the look they've on their face. We then take it so far as to treat them a certain way, vote for them, or form a general opinion about them, all based on this perception we've of them.

Now, I'm not saying that this's right or wrong, but what I'm saying is that it's true. & you can use this truth to your advantage by giving off the impression that you're confident, capable, & easy to get along with. If you carry yourself like a leader, you're going to be treated like a leader.

Chapter 8: Observation

You may not have tried this, but it's perhaps one of the best lessons in body language that you can have. Becoming an observer especially makes you painfully aware of making mistakes with your own body language. People watching is actually becoming a national sport, but for good reason. The examples of body language that people see every day affect their perception & alter the way that they think. Thus, for this exercise, choose a place where there're a lot of people, because you're going to be observing.

Before you go, write down these body language defects which people display, because the observation will show you all of those in action & you'll see firsthand how they affect people's perception of others. These are:

·Twitching·Looking downward
·Playing with hands
·Overly exaggerated hand gestures
·Eye movements·Looking at a watch (showing boredom or impatience)
·Movement of feet
·Crossing arms
·Bodily stance that says "back off"

· **Neediness**

The reason that you're writing these in a notepad is so that you know what you're looking for & you can cross out each one as & when you've understood it & observed it. Observation of these behaviors in other people really helps you to gain a better understanding of what that an action looks like & how you perceived it. It's the best way to stem bad habits & really does show you in real time what these habits do in a social situation.

A busy cafe will usually show you all of these different body language defects & it's quite amusing to observe them because, from this angle you're better able to understand what those signals mean & you can be more conscious about the way that you handle your body when placed in a similar situation.

Another great place to quietly observe a variety of character traits through an observation of body language is the park. Here you can see kids & adults alike & understand how a human mind works, even at such a young age.

You can observe parents sitting around, watching their own children play, & study their body language to gauge what they're feeling. If a parent is continuously looking at the time, you can gauge that they're impatient & cannot wait to leave. If a parent is leaning back onto the bench, with their arms & feet wide apart, you can conclude that they're in a relaxed posture & are probably enjoying the situation as much as their child is & their child is probably an elder child that doesn't need to be looked after constantly. If a parent is on the edge & keeps looking around, you can observe that they're nervous & are ready to jump up at a moment's notice, maybe because they've a naughty child who's often up to no good.

Similarly, observing children is also very helpful. You can observe that how from a very young age we learn how to subconsciously project what's on our mind through our body & even understand the projections of another mind. Observe the children in the middle of the playground who're standing up straight & enjoying themselves. These kids are the leaders of the pack, usually the oldest of the lot & are very confident. Observe the children hanging out at the fringes of the play area. These children aren't very confident & are usually the introverts.

Even the little sand sculptures that the young children make in the sand box can say so much about the children. Those neat & clean sand castles you see? They were made by children who're very organized & like to be perfect. Those lumpy mountains you see? Those're usually made by younger kids who don't have much of a skill.

Even watching a TV show can show you these activities in action, as you watch the body language of actors & actresses & already know the story-line. You can tell, for instance, which people are dishonest, which characters aren't to be trusted, which parts are overly anxious & which interpretations are pushy. These may not be said in words, but you'll know it anyway because the body language even on the TV screen is so clear for viewers to see.

By observing you also get an amazing chance to see your own bad habits in action, even if not being performed by you. Look for boredom, nervousness, self importance, anger, stupidity & all of the things that people display without even uttering a word. These can also be seen clearly simply from the body language displayed. This exercise will help you to recognize your own faults & to list them so that you can practice getting out of the habits that hold you back.

The way forward, when you've problems getting a job or with personal relationships, is to understand what it's that you do that puts people off. Observation will help you to recognize your own faults & will aid you in putting them right. Do you dive into situations in an impetuous way? Doesn't that show lack of professionalism? Think of the kid that does just that & his parents would most certainly slow him down so that he can think of his actions, rather than just simply doing them. Self control is at the very center of correcting your body language, but observation helps you to see what it's you need to control.

Observation isn't just limited to watching people, it's about interpreting what they may or may not be thinking, solely based on what you see & perceive. This will also help you see which habits are an indication of which emotion or which particular aspect of their character & will help you improve yourself.

Chapter 9

Manipulation Through visual communication

Body language can enhance your communication skills during a good way. you'll have effective communication skills, as long as you'll control your visual communication. Before we glance at the foremost used visual communication for manipulation, it's important to understand the way to take hold of your own body. Can we base these with the quote that, 'Charity begins at home'? No, you can't have an interest in understanding the way to manipulate people positively and don't skills to require control of yourself. allow us to begin with understanding and having control of our visual communication.

How to take hold and Manipulate Your visual communication

Research has shown that once you are conscious of the happenings of your own body, you'll manipulate it by training yourself to possess control, and even mound it to possess effective communication. Further research recommends that you simply take some breathing exercises before going into a gathering or presentation. it'll assist you to be calm, also as have the power to require a note of your posture and gestures during the presentation. As you ought to have noted by now, mirroring may be a good technique. Always attempt to be keen on what subsequent person is doing non-verbally and replica that. it'll assist you to become simpler in communicating with them. they're going to understand you better because it enhances your mind with the power to speak more truthfully at an area of relaxation.

However, you ought to take care while shaping your visual communication. you would like to make sure that the visual communication that you simply portray matches with what you're trying to present. A mismatch may bring confusion and should not be relevant now. The person you're in conversation with may misconstrue what you're talking about. the key to having control of your visual communication is to require some time to find out it, to remember of your non-verbal cues, as you apply what you've got learned.

The visual communication which will assist you to take hold of Your Space

Effective management may be a process that involves individuals having the ability to encourage and have a positive influence in planning for a crucial appointment, maybe with their employees, management team, or partners while you're that specialize in what to mention, memorizing critical points, and rehearsing your presentation to form you are feeling believable and persuasive. Of course, this is often something you ought to remember.

Here is what you ought to know if you would like to require control of your position at work when giving a presentation or as a pacesetter.

Seven Seconds is what you've got to form an impact

The first impressions are essential in market relationships. When somebody psychologically marks you as being trustworthy, skeptical, strong, or submissive, you'll be seen through such a filter in the other dealings that you simply do or say. Your partners will want the simplest for you if they such as you. they're going to suspect all of your deeds if they distrust you. And you cannot stop people from having quick decisions. Also, as a defense reaction, the human mind is programmed during a way that you simply can find out how to form these choices effective for you. The initial perceptions are developed and strongly influenced by the visual communication, in but seven seconds. Studies have found that nonverbal signals have quite fourfold the effect on the primary impression you create than you speak. this is often what you ought to know regarding making positive and lasting first impressions. Bear in mind the suggestions highlighted here:

First off, begin by changing your attitude; people immediately devour your mood. have you ever noticed that you simply immediately get turned off after you discover a customer service representative who features a negative attitude? Definitely, you'll desire to leave or request to be served by a special person. That's what happens to anyone with a nasty attitude, which is very noticeable. Consider things and make a deliberate decision about the mindset you'd wish to represent before you meet a client, join the meeting room for a corporation meeting, or tread on the scene to form an analysis.

What about smiling? Smiling may be a good sign used merely by leaders. A smile may be a message, a gesture of recognition and acceptance. "I'm friendly and accessible", it says. Having a smile on your face will change the mood of your audience. If they need another perception of you before, a smile can change that and make them relax.

Make contact together with your eyes. Watching somebody's eyes conveys vitality and expresses interest and transparency. a pleasant thanks to assisting you to make eye contact is to practice observing the attention color of everybody you encounter to reinforce your eye contact. Overcome being shy and practice this great visual communication.

Leaning gently once you are practicing the visual communication that has you leaning forward, often expresses that you simply are actively participating, and you're curious about the discussion. But take care of the space of the opposite individual. This suggests you would like to remain about two ft. away in most professional situations.

Furthermore, shaking hands is that the best and most successful thanks to developing a relationship. Research has found that maintaining the exact same degree of partnership you'll get with an easy handshake takes a minimum of three hours of intense communication. You ought to make sure that you've got palm-to-palm touch which your hold is firm but not bonecrushing.

Look at your position. Studies have found that uniqueness of posture, presenting yourself during a way that exposes your openness and takes up space, generates a way of control that makes changes in behavior during a subject independent of its specific rank or function in a corporation. In fact, in three studies, it had been repeatedly founding that body position was more important than the hierarchical data structure in making an individual think, act, and be viewed more strongly.

Building your credibility depends on how you align your non-verbal communication

Trust is developed by an ideal agreement between what's being said and therefore the accompanying body expressions. If your actions don't completely adhere to your spoken statement, people may consciously or unconsciously interpret dishonesty, confusion, or internal turmoil.

Using an electroencephalograph (EEG) device to calculate "event-related potentials" brain waves that give shape to peaks and valleys to look at gesture effects, proofs that one among these valleys happens when movements that dispute what you say, are shown to subjects. This is often an equivalent dip within the brainwave, which occurs when people hear the language that doesn't add up. Moreover, during a rather reasonable way, they simply don't add up if leaders say one thing and their behaviors point to something else. whenever your facial expressions don't fit your words e.g., losing eye contact or looking everywhere space when trying to precise candour, swaying back on the heels while brooding about the brilliant way forward for the corporate, or locking arms around the chest when announcing transparency. All this causes the verbal message to disappear.

What your hands mean once you use them

Have you at any point seen that when individuals are energetic about what they're stating, their signals naturally end up to be increasingly energized? Their hands and arms constantly move, accentuating focus and spending on eagerness.

You might not have known about this association previously, however, you intuitively felt it. Research shows that an audience will generally view individuals who utilize a more prominent assortment of hand motions during a progressively ideal light. Likewise, studies have found that individuals who convey through dynamic motioning will, generally, be assessed as warm, pleasant, and vivacious, while the individuals who stay still or whose motions appear to be mechanical or "wooden", are viewed as legitimate, cold, and systematic.

That is one motivation behind why signals are so basic to a pioneer's viability and why getting them directly in an introduction associates so effectively with a gaggle of individuals. you would possibly have seen senior administrators commit little avoidable errors. At the purpose when pioneers don't utilize motions accurately on the off chance that they let their hands hang flaccidly to the side, or fasten their hands before their bodies within the exemplary "fig leaf" position, recommends that they need no passionate interest within the issues, or aren't persuaded about the very fact of the matter they're attempting to form.

To utilize signals adequately, pioneers should realize how those developments will altogether probability be seen. Here are four basic hand motions and therefore the messages behind them:

Concealed hands - Shrouded hands do make one look less reliable. This is often one among the nonverbal signs that are profoundly imbued in our subliminal. Our precursors settled on endurance choices hooked into bits of visual data they grabbed from one another. In past, when somebody draws nearer with hands out of view, it indicates potential peril. Albeit today, the danger of shrouded hands is more representative than genuine, and our instilled mental inconvenience remains.

In addition, I've frequently observed that officials utilize the blame game signals in gatherings, arrangements, or meetings for accentuation or to point out strength. the difficulty is that forceful blame dispensing can recommend that the pioneer is losing control of the circumstance and therefore the signal bears a resemblance to parental reprimanding or play area harassing.

Eager gestures - there's an intriguing condition of the hand and arm development with vitality. If you would like to increase more excitement and drive, you'll do intrinsically by expanded motioning. But, overmotioning (particularly when hands are raised over the shoulders) can cause you to look whimsical, less trustworthy, and fewer incredible.

Laidback gestures- Arms held at midsection height, and motions inside that level plane, assist you and therefore the group of spectators, and feel focused and formed. Arms at the midsection and bowed to a 45-degree point (joined by an edge about shoulder-width wide) will likewise assist you with keeping grounded, empowered, and centered.

In this quick-pace, techno-charged time of email, writings, video chats, and video visits, but one generally accepted fact remains; face-to-confront is that the most liked, gainful, and amazing correspondence medium. The more business pioneers conveyed electronically, the more squeezing turns into the need for individual communication.

Here's the reason:

In face to face gatherings, our brain processes the nonstop course of nonverbal signs that we use because of the reason for building trust and expert closeness. Eye-to-eye collaboration is data-rich. We translate what individuals tell us just halfway from the words they use. We get an outsized portion of the message (and the bulk of the passionate subtlety behind the words) from vocal tone, pacing, outward appearances, and other nonverbal signs. Moreover, we rely on prompt input of the fast reactions of others to help us with checking how well our thoughts are being acknowledged.

The nonverbal connection between people is robust that once we are in certified affinity with them, we subliminally coordinate our body positions, developments, and even our breathing rhythms with theirs. Most intriguing, in up close and private experiences, the mind's "reflect neurons" impersonate practices, yet sensations and sentiments too. At some extent, once we are denied of this relational promptness and are compelled to depend upon the printed or verbally expressed word alone, the cerebrum battles and genuine correspondence endures.

Innovation is often an excellent facilitator of factual data, but meeting people is the key to positive relationships between employees and clients. Whatever industry you're employed in, business individuals are always involved. However, regardless of how tech-savvy you'll be, face-to-face gatherings are far and away from the foremost successful way of capturing attendees' interest, engaging them during a discussion, and fostering fruitful teamwork. it's said that if it doesn't matter that much, send an email. If it's crucial for the task, but not significant, make a call. If it's extremely important for the success of the project, it's advised to travel see someone.

Ability to review visual communication

More business administrators are learning the way to send the right sign, and the way to know them. the foremost significant thing in correspondence is hearing what isn't said.

Correspondence occurs in additional than two channels: verbal and nonverbal, bringing about two unmistakable discussions simultaneously. While verbal correspondence is critical. it's by all account, not the sole message sent. Without the capacity to read non-verbal communication, we miss critical components to discussions which will emphatically or adversely sway a business.

At the purpose when individuals aren't occupied by an activity, pioneers should have the choice to perceive what's happening and react rapidly. this is often why commitment and withdrawal are two of the foremost significant signs to screen in individuals' non-verbal communication. Commitment practices demonstrate intrigue, receptivity, or understanding, while separation practices signal fatigue, outrage, or protectiveness.

A sign of active participation sign incorporates head gestures or tilts the widespread indication of "giving somebody your ear", and open body poses. At the purpose when individuals are locked in, they're going to confront you straightforwardly, "pointing" at you with their entire body. Nevertheless, the instant they feel awkward, they'll edge their chest area away – supplying you with ignore." Moreover, if they endure the entire gathering with the 2 arms and legs crossed, it's far-fetched that you simply have their upfront investment.

Additionally, screen the measure of eye-to-eye connection that you simply want to be involved. Generally, individuals will stare longer and with more recurrence at individuals or things that they like. an outsized number folks accept the eye-to-eye connection enduring around three seconds, yet once we like or concur with somebody, we consequently increment the measure of your time we investigate their eyes. Separation triggers the inverse; the measure of eye-to-eye connection diminishes, as we'll generally shy away from things that trouble or get us bored.

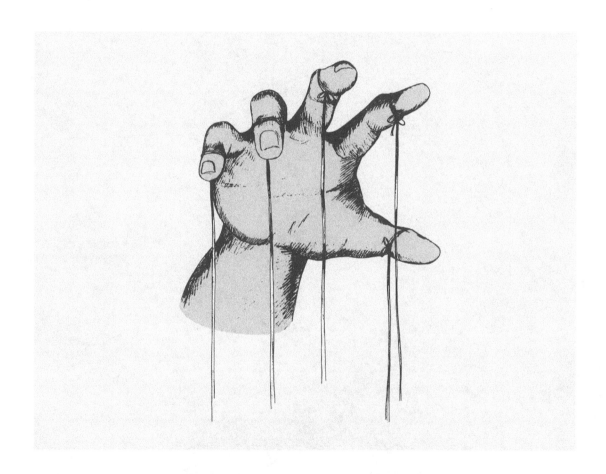

Chapter 10

Use of visual communication

Your visual communication is beneficial in many various ways. When used well, it can add your favor. one among these areas is being very effective in negotiation. you ought to note that, in negotiation, you're trying to convince the opposite person to comply with your terms. Allow us to discuss more.

Negotiation Skills

Negotiation may be a way of achieving agreement by a discussion between individuals. it's a mechanism that reaches consensus and determination by preventing conflicts and disputes.

People attempt to create the simplest possible result for his or her role or perhaps an entity they represent in any conflict. However, the concepts of honesty are the keys to having a successful result, trying to hunt mutual affection and keeping a connection. In many circumstances, specific sorts of bargaining are getting used as examples, diplomacy, the judiciary, administration, industrial conflicts, or domestic partnerships. During a big variety of activities, specific negotiating skills are often learned and implemented. It might be helpful to pursue a scientific approach for negotiation to accomplish a positive outcome. as an example, a gathering might get to be organized during a work environment during which all parties involved will close.

The negotiation process contains the subsequent steps:

- Preparedness
- Discussion

- Elaboration of Objectives
- Compromise towards a Win/win result
- Common understanding
- Execution of an action plan

Now allow us to see what each step contains.

Preparedness

Before any conversation takes place, a choice has got to be made on when and where a gathering is going to be held to debate the difficulty and who are going to be involved. Setting a limited timescale can also be helpful in preventing the dispute from continuing. This step involves ensuring that you simply are conscious of all the relevant circumstances to clarify your position. From the above instance, the workplace was found out in a neighbourhood which will include recognizing the principles of the corporate to whom assistance is provided, when assistance is not needed, and therefore the reasons for such refusals. the corporate may need procedures that you simply can ask within the negotiation plan. Preparing before resolving the conflict will help to avoid further conflict and unnecessarily wasting of your time during the meeting.

Discussion

In this process, people or members of every party put the case forward as they see it, i.e. their interpretation of the matter. Throughout this phase, core skills include examining, listening, and clarification.

Apart from that, it's sometimes helpful to require notes of all the points suggests, to recollect if further clarity is required. Hearing is critical; it's simple to form the error of taking an excessive amount of and hearing far less when there's a misunderstanding. There should be a civil right for every side to plead their case.

Clarification of Objectives

It is necessary to elucidate the goals, desires, and viewpoints of the 2 sides involved within the conflict from the discussion. Listing these components grouped by need is extremely helpful. Moreover, identifying and fixing certain common beliefs are often possible through this process. Clarification may be a vital piece of the arrangement process. However, it's possible that incorrect expectations will arise which will cause problems or challenges to realize a useful outcome, without it.

Negotiation Towards a Win-Win Outcome

This phase focuses on what's considered a 'win-win outcome'; where the 2 sides feel that they need to be picked up something good through the agreement process, which their viewpoint has been overlapped. Generally, the simplest result's a win-win result. While this might not necessarily be possible, it should be a particular objective through the agreement. Elective methodology and bargaining proposals should be considered at this stage. Bargains are routinely constructive options which will often obtain benefits that are more influential for all concerned, withholding from the primary positions as compared.

Agreement

Comprehension is often achieved once the grasp of the viewpoints and concerns of the 2 sides are taken under consideration. it's important for all needed to stay a responsive attitude to realize an adequate agreement. the choice should be made perfectly clear in order that the 2 parties will know what was chosen.

Execution of An Action Plan

After going during the steps, it'll reach some extent where the choice has got to be made. Therefore, the action takes place.

Now, allow us to discuss the highest negotiation skills which will offer you a whip hand.

In their very own curiosity, some people are excellent at negotiating, while some aren't. Which one among these sorts of people would you wish to be? Answer that yourself, as you read through. one among your primary jobs in nature is to be more successful in manipulating others, by acquiring great negotiating skills and selecting appropriate inquiries to ask. We consider that they need equivalent attributes in many of the researches done by successful negotiators.

Negotiation Skills are often Nurtured

In spite of prevalent thinking, top negotiators aren't hard bargainers and extreme firm of characters. they're not forceful, pushy, and don't request express demands. they do not constrain their partners in negotiation into unacceptable understandings. the simplest arbitrators are perpetually charming individuals. they're warm, benevolent, amicable, pleasing and low-keyed. they're the type of people that you simply feel good being in concord. you've got a practically programmed inclination to open up to somebody with incredible exchange abilities and to feel that their request is going to be of the best advantage of the 2 parties.

Top Negotiation Skills

Talented mediators are generally very worried about finding a solution or a course of action that's agreeable to the 2 gatherings. They look for the "winwin" circumstances, where the 2 gatherings are contented with the impact of the exchange. In consulting with any kind of agreement within the case of buying or selling anything, there are some fundamental skills in a negotiation that you simply need to learn to urge the simplest arrangement for yourself and to feel cheerful about the result. allow us to look deeply into these skills.

Pick Good inquiries to Ask

Great mediators appear to pose plenty of inquiries and are worried about knowing what you're attempting to accomplish from the arrangement.

For instance, in purchasing a house, the 2 gatherings may begin contending and differing over the value. they begin with the proposition that the value is that the most vital thing of all, and that they must negotiate well upon it. In any case, the talented negotiator will understand that cost is simply one piece of the bundle. Moreover, by utilizing great abilities in negotiation, this arbitrator will assist the 2 gatherings by seeing that the particulars of the deal are additionally significant, almost like the furnishings and apparatuses which will be involved within the exchange. Exploring wonderful inquiries to pose, regarding the present needs of a customer, is that the primary way during which you'll have the choice to seek out out, during a negotiation forum, exactly what's crucial for them and what benefits they're truly trying to find. Price is typically not the foremost important thing during a contract, and it's imperative to offer the buyer different benefits that they're hospitable receiving.

The Act of Patience

Good negotiators ' act of persistence is extremely cautious. It relies on reaching a consensus on all aspects of the agreement that are related between the 2 sides before they proceed to look for nice ways to unravel other problems. They always spend time to pose great inquiries to get clarification and understanding on each topic as they are going along, in order that there'll be no ambiguity within the nearest future.

Planning is vital

Planning is liable for 90% achievement made. The more found out made preceding an appointment, the more probable it's that the results of the exchange are going to be palatable for all gatherings included.

Preparation requires you to finish two things. First, get all the info that you simply can about the up and coming arrangement. Secondly, consider the exchange cautiously from the beginning to the top, and be completely arranged for any projection.

The first data you would like is about the item or administration, and therefore the individual with whom you'll arrange. You get this data by picking great inquiries to pose that each condition is taken into account. during this sense, data become a kind of intensity, and therefore the power is consistently on the individual with the simplest data.

Make a Move and Gain Self-Confidence!

It is important to understand that nothing elevates your boldness faster than knowing that you've got been successful in negotiating a contract and you have got an honest arrangement accordingly. Furthermore, nothing will reduce your self-assurance quicker than thinking that you've got been out consulted during a bad situation you'd need to affect. Trying to rearrange skills and skills is, therefore, a crucial a part of your development of character, and sense of private viability and self-assurance.

When you are an honest arbitrator, your fearlessness is lowered, and you are feeling increasingly optimistic about yourself and people in everything you are doing.

How to Negotiate Through visual communication

As we start this significant topic, allow us to start from what experts within the negotiation watch from you. Skilled negotiators have learned to read visual communication and to require advantage of the resulting observations. this may help in aligning your skills.

Recognize the start line

To read the visual communication of your counterpart correctly, you would like to first evaluate the suitable behaviour of that individual or point of reference. once you don't spend the time to try to just that, you're likely to misunderstand the signs portrayed. "Baselining", which suggests watching individuals once they aren't experiencing periods of distress or stress which will cause them to possess a short-lived change of non-verbal cues. Having a baseline will assist you to know their normal behaviour. It only involves several moments to possess a way of how anyone behaves during a comfortable or neutral atmosphere, and therefore the best time to try to that's before the negotiation begins. for instance, when having lunch and making "chitchat." While you're talking unofficially, ask a couple of basic questions that you simply already know the answers to (and there wouldn't be an excuse for lying). Then watch how your counterpart behaves when being relaxed and candid. it's advisable to; Check what proportion eye contact is granted to you. to notice when the eyes attend one preferred direction while making true answers, to verify if they're smiling along with the method. make sure that it's a real smile. Also, check what expressions you'll see most frequently. If your partner is comfortable, what quite pose is exhibited?

After you've got established how your counterpart utilizes their body while during a comfortable or unofficial context, you'll have a baseline against which you'll start comparing significant body-language variances during the method of negotiation.

Track the many Cues

The most essential cues to trace within the other person's visual communication in any negotiation are their commitment, disconnection, and depression. Behaviours of participation (eye contact, head nods, smiles, leaning forward, etc.), imply interest, openness, or consent. The behaviours that show that one isn't engaged to, include looking away, leaning back, eyes closed, frowns, and far more, which suggest that a private is bored, frustrated, or defensive. Cues of pressure include a high vocal tone, facetouching, and closely crossed feet, which are most frequently related to playing dumb and frustration because the negotiation continues.

Check the Group of Gestures

Nonverbal prompts happen in what's referred to as a bunch of gestures, which may be a gathering of developments, stances, and activities that strengthen a typical point. an effort to disentangle non-verbal communication from a solitary expression resembles attempting to get and analyze the meaning of a narrative, during a single word. you ought to note that, when words show up in sentences or motions in bunches, their importance progresses toward becoming clearer. as an example, a person's squirming might not mean much without anyone else, if that individual is maintaining a strategic distance from eye-to-eye connection by wringing his hands, and guiding his feet to the entryway, you'll wager he's troubled and wishes to go away. an honest rule is to look for 3 non-verbal communication flags that fortify the equivalent nonverbal message.

Take attention on the Environment

A non-verbal cue is often profoundly very essential or makes no difference by any means. It relies mostly upon the setting where that signal is shown. allow us to take an example of arms crossed; during a crowd of individuals, I hope to ascertain individuals with their arms crossed sitting within the battlefront. I realize that without a line of seats before them, many of us will make a blockade with their arms in any event initially , before they get won't to the speaker and convey down their defences. In like manner, if your arrangement accomplice is sitting during a seat that does not have armrests, understand that the restricted alternative improves the probability of crossed arms – because the reaction will drop-in temperature.

This is additionally the rationale why baselining is so significant. Somebody who sits with crossed arms when loose or keen is sending an altogether different message than somebody whose first show of that signal comes following your request for a counteroffer. This, obviously, would be particularly significant if different signs joined the crossed arms. as an example, decreased eye-to-eye connection and shoulders that unpretentiously were directed faraway from you.

There will consistently be parts of the environmental setting that you simply won't realize. A firm pose could be a sign of an intense negotiation position or it'd demonstrate a solid back.

Moreover, it'd appear to be an unimaginable assignment, particularly when you will be leading a discussion simultaneously. However, recollect that you've got been reading non-verbal communication for your entire life.

Presently, all that's distinctive is that you are taking this inborn, yet oblivious ability into mindfulness –thereby learning understanding into what your arranging partner is actually thinking.

Chapter 11

Guide to Effective visual communication

Body language is diverse. Just to make sure that you simply don't portray different non-verbal communications, it's important to find out effective visual communication. during this chapter, we'll emphasize that and more.

Seven of the foremost Significant Hints for Successful Non-Verbal Communication ahead of an Audience

Deal with Your Feeling of hysteria

While you're standing by at the rear of the stage, see the pressure in your body. Understand that some apprehensive vitality is some things worth being thankful for. Though it's what makes your introduction exuberant and interesting, however, tons of pressure brings about nonverbal practices which will challenge you.

Before you enter front of an audience, stand, or sit together with your weight focused and equally disseminated on the 2 feet or seat bones. Look ahead while that specialize in your jawline level to the ground and relax your throat. Take a couple of profound "paunch" breaths. Take count gradually to 6, as you inhale and out the strain in your body by making some fists and straining the muscles in your middle arms and legs. As you exhale, permit your hands, arms, and body to relax and unwind.

Express Emotions

To attract a crowd of individuals, they ought to be genuinely included. So, before you enter front of an audience to convey your message, specialise in feelings and sentiments. How would you get a genuine interface with what you're getting to state? what's your feeling towards it? How would you like a gaggle of spectators to feel? The more you centre on the sensation behind your message, the even more persuading and harmonious your non-verbal communication will consequently become.

Get in confidently

Remain very relaxed, leave the stage with an excellent stance, head held high, and an everlasting smooth stride. At the purpose, once you land within the middle of everyone's attention, stop grinning, cause a stir, and somewhat broaden your eyes while you inspect the space. A casual, open face and body tell your group of spectators that you're sure and okay with the info you're conveying. Since a gaggle of spectating individuals will answer any showcase of pressure, your condition of solace will likewise unwind and console them. this might appear to be the presence of mind, yet I once worked with a director who strolled ahead of an audience with slouched shoulders, wrinkled temples, and squinted eyes. I viewed the group of spectators squirm accordingly. it had been a disrupting approach to start out a "how about we get together and bolster this change?" discourse.

Keep in Touch

Keep in touch with the gang during the discussion. On the off chance that you simply will rapidly prefer to not be there, that you simply aren't generally dedicated to your message, or that you simply have something to hide up.

While it's physically difficult to stay in-tuned with the entire crowd constantly, you'll take a gander at explicit people or little gatherings, hold their consideration quickly, and afterwards move to a different gathering or individual in another a part of the space.

Dodge the Platform

Whenever things allow, get out from behind the platform. a robust podium doesn't just conceal most of your body; it additionally goes about as a boundary among you and therefore the group of spectators. Practice the introduction so well that you simply wouldn't get to peruse from a content. On the off chance that you simply use notes, demand a video guide at the foot of the stage.

Converse together with your Hands

Speakers use hand signals to underscore what's significant, and to precise emotions, needs and feelings. At the purpose when individuals are hooked into what they're stating, their motions become progressively enlivened. Those are the explanations signals are so basic and why getting them directly in introduction interfaces so intensely with a crowd of individuals. within the event that you simply don't utilize them (probably that you let your hands hang flaccidly to your sides or fasten them within the exemplary "fig leaf" position), it recommends you do not perceive the vital issues, you've got no enthusiasm for the problems, or that you are not a viable communicator.

Move

Individuals people most particularly are interested in shifting. Moving sideby-side shields a crowd of individuals from being exhausted. It tends to be compelling to walk toward the group of spectators before making a big point, and away once you got to flag an opportunity or a difference within the subject. However, don't move once you are making a key point. Rather, stop, enlarge your position, and convey that significant message.

Walking Styles

A ton of knowledge is passed on not just by how you stand or how you talk, but by how you progress. the design of strolling passes on plenty of knowledge about our fearlessness and our characteristics. this is often one motivation behind why the non-verbal communication mentors show strolling styles to their understudies.

Stand Straight and confront

The primary thing to recollect is that you simply ought to not slump or hunch while strolling. the rear must be straight, and therefore the spine must be erect. Your head must be upstanding, and your eyes must take a gander at the front. The jaw must be up constantly. many of us look down while taking a walk. this is not taken to be exquisite. Besides, if you slacken or hunch while strolling, you'll be viewed as being powerless and bereft of vitality and energy.

Terrible stance while strolling, whenever preceded for extended timeframes, can prompt back agony, hardened neck, and different genuine sicknesses.

Utilize All Muscles

It is advised to utilize all of your muscle bunches within the legs while strolling. While strolling, plan to picture pushing off together with your back foot, utilizing your hamstrings and quadriceps, and propelling yourself forward on to the impact point of the opposite foot. plan to move your foot forward, impact point to toe. This causes the lower leg muscles to figure and encourages you to stay your feet at the proper fringe of each progression.

Pull Back the Shoulders

The next thing to recollect is to stay the shoulders pulled back, yet loose. Keeping a pulled back yet loosened up position of shoulders, keeps up a gentle and vertical segment of help while walking, alongside the straight back and jawline up pose, which makes strolling diminish the chances of injury. This stance additionally radiates certainty and quality.

While strolling, the chest area must become possibly the foremost important factor alongside the legs. The arms got to swing appropriately to increase certainty; they need to move during a littler circular segment as you walk. The quicker you walk, the larger the circular segment you create. the event of arms increases a superior walk.

Get the proper Speed

The pace of the walk likewise matters an excellent deal. While strolling, the pace must be to such an extent that you simply can talk appropriately to a private while proceeding together with your walk and ought to not seem winded simultaneously.

Walking shrewdly additionally includes not accepting too long walks as you walk. Protracting the walk extends the leg muscles pointlessly and prompts destabilization of the walk. Research has discovered that a touch swag of the shoulders features a particular kind of sex-request associated with it.

While having a walk, the hips must be at level, and therefore the means must be of equivalent length. you ought to twist your arms at 90 degrees at the elbow and swing appropriately with the contrary leg. This aid in learning the balance while strolling. The knees must point forward, and therefore the pelvis should be tucked under the centre. additionally, the top ought to not be tilted and will be held high. Putting your heel on the bottom first and not the toe is that the penultimate thing to try to to.

Positive visual communication and Its Significance

In the corporate world, maintaining great non-verbal communication assumes a big job. Great non-verbal communication is acknowledged and energized within the corporate division. Awful non-verbal communication leaves the individuals during a breakdown of the company arrangements and furthermore, a number of the time organizes misfortune.

Indeed, even without eager to show the emotions, the emotions and feelings are often shared and imparted by the stance of the body, alongside the body developments. This demonstrates the old saying "Actions speak louder than voices".

A portion of the perspectives where positive non-verbal communication demonstrates to be significant is as per the following:

Self-Assured Behavior

An individual finishes up being fearless and assured by joining positive non-verbal communication. Constructive non-verbal communication empowers the individual to expire the info and conclusion during a progressively straightforward way. Numerous individuals enjoy the emphatic conduct of constructive non-verbal communication and during this way; individuals with constructive non-verbal communication attract more individuals.

Non-Verbal Communication

As indicated by the investigations, it's viewed that correspondence includes 65% non-verbal and 35% verbal. It infers that the opposite individual sees just 35% through words, and therefore the remaining 65% is seen by the nonverbal communication. The way of life, feelings and therefore the status of a private is distinguished by the non-verbal communication.

Thus, non-verbal correspondence is critical than verbal correspondence. Non-verbal correspondence encourages rehashing the message, restricting the words, underpinning the announcements, and replacing the sentence meaning, which may provide a significant base to the words. More so, it's significant that non-verbal communication needs to accept as true with the emotions and feelings. There ought to not be any inclination of crisscross between the non-verbal communication and verbal correspondence. this might establish other individuals under the connection that the individual is misleading.

Working Environment Success

In a professional workplace, it's extremely fundamental to possess positive non-verbal communication. It helps in upgrading the representative soul by a build-up working environment cooperation. Positive non-verbal communication streamlines the procedure of assignment and empowers to work out the contentions.

A portion of the parts of constructive non-verbal communication, for instance, inclining forward, open palms, tenderly grin and direct eye-to-eye connection helps in creating relations with different individuals, particularly in gatherings and subsequently results in a solid association with all of the individuals engaged with the gathering.

Connections

The relations with different individuals could be ruined by odd developments of the body and therefore the body acts during this manner, prompting confound and misconstruing the connection and individual.

The conduct with a private relies upon the emotions and temperament of the opposite individual. for instance, if a companion is during a positive mindset, then prodding or pulling the legs are going to be taken by the companion as sportive and fun, but similar conduct could also be confused as bad-tempered conduct if the companion isn't feeling great.

Open Speaking

In an open talk, care needs to be taken regarding non-verbal communication. If non-verbal communication is either cautious or latent, it'd prompt lose the keenness for the group of spectators for the discourse. during this way, the effect of the discourse additionally is diminished. this is often because the group of spectators and therefore the rest 65% (nonverbal) is passed up an excellent opportunity by the gang are becoming solitary 35% of the correspondence (verbal correspondence). last, in open communication, positive non-verbal communication demonstrates to be extremely fundamental.

Chapter 12 .Detecting Lying and Deception

There are signals that we send only in a certain situation. If you only knew what your subconscious mind is doing, it is worthwhile to find a genetically appropriate specimen (read: handsome or pretty). But before that, we will deal with another interesting problem: what happens to our subconscious when we try to lie.

A person who claims to be able to read minds and analyze others should notice when they lie to him. You have already learned to recognize the signs of falsehood and to guess from the face, whether a person is lying or telling the truth. But the most difficult thing you have to master.

The easiest way to lie is in words. We do this throughout our lives. It is harder to lie using facial expressions, although many people do it well. But the most difficult thing is to lie with your whole being (or body). We do not think about it, but the body has its own language and often says what it wants, and not what we intended. In conversation, people pay attention primarily to words, less often to facial expressions and almost never to the body of the interlocutor.

When we suspect a person of lying, we carefully listen to his words, instead of paying attention to the tone of his voice or body language. But this is the only way to check whether a person is lying or not. In fact, we see the signals of the excitement that he is experiencing (and when he lies too). He may be nervous, not because he is lying, but for another reason. There are signals that mean a lie and only a lie—and we need to learn to distinguish. Some people are well versed in lies and its various manifestations. Others circle the finger easy. There are congenital liars for whom lying is like breathing. They do not send any signals and usually refer to psychopaths. There are people who do not know how to lie. We are all different. But most of us send signals that can be learned to distinguish.

What is a lie?

The ability to recognize lies has always been admired by people. Without this skill, it is difficult to work in the police or in court. The testimony of the classic "lie detector" is sometimes erroneous, so many scientists, including Paul Ekman, spent so much time and effort to learn to recognize a lie, and in part, they succeeded. But first, let's think about what a lie is.

Most people lie all the time, or rather, their words do not quite accurately reflect reality. This is how our society and culture are organized, where lies are accepted. To the question "How are you?" The person answers "Good," he does not talk about his problems, because the other person is not interested in the interlocutor and in fact, he is just being polite.

There are situations when people are forced to lie and hide their thoughts. At a beauty contest, the winner may sob from excitement, while the losing participants are forced to smile and pretend to be happy for her. If a lie was not accepted in our society, the participants of the beauty contest would sob bitterly and something else, they would have pulled the finalist by the hair. Do not show your true feelings—this is a kind of lie.

Of course, these forms of lies do not interest us. We are interested in when people lie not out of politeness or on sociocultural motives, but on their own initiative — consciously, knowing that things that do not correspond to reality. Remember, lies are not only the lies that we speak but also the truth about which we are silent. If I say that I won a tennis match, which I actually lost, then I lie. If I say that I am having fun, but in fact I am sad, I lie.

When someone lies, he does it out of fear of punishment or in the hope of reward. Our lies always have a reason. There is also a combination of these two motives: when we want to receive an undeserved reward, but if a lie is revealed, a fine is waiting for us. For example, everyone will know that we have lied—this is also a punishment to some extent.

Conflicting Signals

A person gives false signals only when the reason becomes a very significant factor when a person risks something when he is worried. And it is the excitement that is reflected on his face—the feeling that we can read as a sign of lies. First, you need to find all the signals, and then correctly interpret them. In the case of a lie, there are always two messages: truthful and deceitful, both equally important, we must learn to distinguish between them. The message comes not only from our words but also from the whole body—all the tools that combine under the name "non-verbal communication" are used. Therefore, we are talking about how skillfully a person hides a truthful message and gives a lie for the truth. It is about selfcontrol (that is, control over emotions and reactions). As is the case with the meaning of a facial expression, a person tries to disguise one feeling with another. To understand whether he is lying or not, you need to follow the channels of communication that are the most difficult to control. A person who speaks the truth unconsciously sends similar signals, but if we feel a symbolic discrepancy between words and facial expressions of a person or movements of his hands, then we can talk about lies. This is what I mean by "conflicting signals." We say one thing, think the other, and do the third. And the easiest way, of course, is to control your words.

American psychologist Robert Trivers came up with a solution to the problem for all professional liars. You just need to convince yourself that a lie is true. Then all of our signals, conscious and unconscious, will carry the same message.

But such manipulations of consciousness carry health risks. Inconsistent signals are often referred to as unconscious leakage or simply leakage. You may think that it's great to hide your feelings, but people are able to mask only obvious, obvious signs. Anyway, there is an unconscious leak, which is also unconsciously perceived by another person (this means that people notice this, not really aware of what they are doing).

When a person lies, he cannot control all the signals that his body sends, and he will surely give himself away. But there are also pathological liars who don't betray themselves, with such you have to be especially careful. So the absence of leakage is still not a guarantee that they tell you the truth. In addition, sometimes for a leak, we can take the usual behavior of a person who is not well known. That is why it is important to note whether the signals are the result of a change in a person's normal behavior. It is necessary to carefully monitor his reactions and only then draw the appropriate conclusions.

If the interlocutor sends a number of conflicting signals, it is highly likely that he is lying. It may also mean that he is trying to hide his true feelings. Often it is easy to check. Following the methods outlined, do not forget that the signals can be sent by a person whose thoughts during your conversation are simply busy with something else. None of these methods gives an absolute guarantee. Always pay attention to the context and try not to make hasty conclusions. And in general: is it important for you if this person is lying or not?

Controversial Body Language

The clearest signals are given by our nervous system. It is very difficult for us to control them. It's almost impossible to force yourself to stop sweating or blush when you worry. Unable to control pupils at the poker table. But our nervous system reacts only in the case of very strong emotions, —then what to do if a lie does not cause a person to be very excited?

Face

A person's face always expresses two states: feelings that he is ready to show to others, and his true thoughts, which he does not want to share with anyone. Sometimes these two states coincide, but this happens extremely rarely. If we try to manage our facial expressions, we do it in three ways.

• Qualification – We add to the existing facial expression another (forexample, we depict a smile to hide the sadness).

• Simulation – We change the intensity of the expressions on the face,making them more or less bright. This is achieved through the activity of the facial muscles and the period of time in which they are involved.

• Falsification (simulation) – We show feelings that we really don'tfeel. There are other options, for example, we try not to give out our feelings (neutralization) or disguise them as others (disguise).

In order for others to believe us, we must have good control of the muscles of the face. This is especially possible for children who with pleasure "make faces" in front of a mirror. With age, this ability deteriorates, so we often have no idea how we look in a given situation. Sometimes we simply do not have time to prepare, and we do everything as if in the hope that this will "give a smooth ride".

The most difficult thing is to neutralize your feelings, to pretend that you do not feel them, especially if these feelings are strong and sincere. Often a person (against the will of a person) turns into a mask, and the interlocutor immediately realizes that there is something wrong, and tries to find out what is being hidden from him. Therefore liars prefer to mask one feeling with another. You already know that in disguise, we mainly use the lower part of the face. This means that our eyes, eyebrows, and forehead give out our true state.

Another, the most common way to disguise is a smile. Charles Darwin had a whole theory about it. He said that most often we strive to disguise negative emotions, and with a smile, there are completely different muscles that are easy to control at that moment.

A sincere smile is always symmetrical: both corners of the mouth simultaneously lift up. A fake smile may well be asymmetrical (one corner of the mouth is raised). A smile at one corner of the mouth can also speak of contempt or disgust for the interlocutor. A genuinely smiling man smiles not only with his lips but with his eyes too.

Actors, to seem sincere, try before you smile, remember something pleasant so that the joy was real. It should also be remembered that a real smile, unlike a fake one, does not appear suddenly: a person needs time to realize the joy. But to portray a lie, just one pulse.

Micro-expressions play a big role when you need to guess the state of the interlocutor. Sometimes the other person smiles and says nice things, and we feel that there is something wrong here. Most likely, our subconscious noted micro facial expressions and correctly interpreted them. The only pity is that not all people show micro-expressions or show them when they are trying to suppress emotions, and not to lie.

They say that a liar can be recognized by the eyes. Recall the expression: "I see in your eyes that you're lying." There is a statement: if a person looks away or blinks often, he lies. Perhaps there is some truth in this. But people are so sure of this phenomenon that now that they are lying, they are trying to look their interlocutor right in the eyes. Since childhood, we have heard that a liar is afraid to look into his eyes, but unfortunately, this will not help us now. There are situations when we look to the side for natural reasons: for example, we look down, when we are sad, to the side—when we are ashamed, or we look through a person when he is unpleasant. The most experienced liars are those who can look away in time.

Excitement also gives the size of the pupils. They expand with excitement or wonder. Listen to the person and watch his pupils at the same time. If he tells you something important, his pupils cannot remain the same.

When a liar blinks, his eyes usually remain closed longer than in an honest person. The British zoologist Desmond Morris, who studied the behavior of animals and people, noticed that this happens, for example, during police interrogation. This is an unconscious human attempt to escape from reality, as does an ostrich, burying its head in the sand.

It is also important to monitor eye movements. Remember what I told you about memories and the design of new thoughts? When designing, we use our imagination, and we need it when we think about the future, create something new, invent fairy tales, and so on. Depending on whether we are remembering something or creating a new thought, our eyes move in different ways. A lie is also a construction because we are creating something that was not there. If a visual talks about something and claims that he has seen everything with his own eyes, and at the same time his gaze is directed upwards to the right, it means that he is inventing (constructing) everything. Then ask yourself: why should he invent something? For example, a person tells you: "I stayed at work and was very hungry. Then I ate pizza with Jock and immediately went home. " If at the words "I ate pizza with Jock" a person looks up to the right, then he is making it up. Something is wrong here. It is possible that he blatantly lies.

A person cannot control his view, which, while constructing, against his will, will be directed upwards to the right, which is why a liar cannot look directly into his eyes, but if a person tells you what really was the place to be, that is, he remembers, he may look you in the eye. This means that if a person had time to invent a lie, speak it to himself, maybe even memorize it, then he can calmly repeat it (remember), looking straight into your eyes. In this case, it does not matter whether he tells about a real event or all this is the fruit of his fantasy. Do not forget that not all people fit this model. It is worth thinking ten times before letting out to spend the night with an unfamiliar person, no matter what he tells you.

Arms

It is more difficult to control the face than other parts of the body because the activity of the facial muscles is associated with brain function. But we are often betrayed by other parts of the body, such as hands. Our hands can give a variety of signals. As in the case of words, a certain gesture has a certain meaning (emblem), understood by all representatives of the same culture. For example, Winston Churchill's gesture in the form of the Latin letter V, formed by two fingers, means victory, and all representatives of Western civilization know this. Lie gestures easier than ever. It is only necessary to answer the question "Did you win the match?" By lifting up two fingers. Even if in fact we brutally lost.

Sometimes we use gestures unconsciously, and they can tell us what a person really thinks and feels because he does not control them. Detecting them is not easy. Paul Ekman, for example, discovered a gesture that students made during a conversation with an unpleasant person. Unconsciously, they clenched their hands into a fist, sometimes even exposing one finger, as if showing the interviewer an indecent gesture. But this happened under the table, and this person still could not see him. There was no doubt that with a gesture the students express disgust for the interlocutor, although they do not realize that they are experiencing precisely this feeling.

Another well-known gesture is shrugging when we want to show our ignorance or that we don't care. The shoulders are raised, and, accordingly, the hands, too, palms are usually aimed at the other person.

There are also hand movements with which we illustrate our statements (for example, we outline the contours in the air, speaking of abstract concepts). All people use their hands when talking, only the activity of gestures varies from one culture to another. For example, southern Europeans—Italians and Spaniards—are very fond of accompanying their words with intensive gestures. We rarely pay attention to gestures, but in fact, they mean a lot to us.

It is impossible to communicate with a person who says one thing and shows something completely different from his hands. In my seminars, I am doing the following experiment. I look man directly in the eye, ask how much time it is, and at the same time point the finger at the window. In response, I always get: "Um ... What?", although, it would seem that there can be no simpler question. True, there are cases when the use of gestures is minimized—for example, at the moment of fatigue, when we do not have the strength or we are bored or sad, and if we focus heavily on the words of the interlocutor.

Creating new thoughts is a complex mental process. Focusing on the invention of the new, we forget about gestures. Our body is practically not involved, only the speech apparatus works. The absence of gestures is a sure sign that a person is lying.

When I ask how a liar can be identified, people usually respond that he often scratches his nose. There is some truth in this. People who lie tend to hold their hands to their faces, but scratching the nose is not so common. You will be surprised, but quite often the liars cover their mouths with their hands as if they do not let the words of untruth fly from their tongues or are ashamed of what they are lying. If a person covers his mouth with his hand while talking to you, scratches his nose, constantly adjusts his glasses, tugs at the earlobe, he most likely lies.

All these gestures can sometimes be seen from someone who just sits and listens to another. Agree, we often keep silent about our true thoughts and do not speak in person to the interlocutor that, in our opinion, he lies. If you have noticed such signs in the person with whom you speak, try to convey your thoughts more clearly to convince him of the truth of what was said. You do not want to be considered a deceiver?

Like all other signs, scratching the nose does not necessarily give the person a brazen liar. But if your interlocutor scratched his nose several times during a conversation, it is worth looking for other signs of lying or silencing the truth.

Chapter 13

Understanding People Through visual communication

You may be wondering why it's important to find out other people's visual communication. it's going to be a challenge, but it's important that you simply are aware. the power to know other people's visual communication saves you tons of your time that you simply would have probably been researching why they did something. This chapter dwells on how you'll understand people through visual communication.

Identifying People's Hidden Thoughts Through visual communication

To gain the art of understanding people's non-verbal communication may be a hard thing. you'll be wondering how you'll specialize in learning other people's cues while you are doing not even know yourself fully. Well, the book would assist you to demystify the art of understanding visual communication for various people.

All folks are subconscious experts in interpreting the thoughts of other individuals around us. within the northern mammoth age, we developed these abilities since our life trusted them, and therefore the unconscious would work more efficiently than the conscious mind. However, once we make this unconscious understanding conscious, it doesn't yield an honest result. Practically, we will respond with lightning speed to dodge a fist that some whiny brat throws in our way, or to leap out from the way of an approaching car, before we will believe it explicitly.

It's great; it's subconscious, and it works. But especially, we discover that the majority of folks are much less skilled at actively knowing what everyone else during a group is thinking, doing, or determining. as an example, knowing if the chief ringleaders within the group are against your growth plan or not. There are those motives to ascertain, within the language of the body. the difficulty is that we simply get such a lot faraway from insufficient data of what others decide to do. People move, shake, continuously attempt to search, down or sideways, raise their eyebrows, roll their eyes, close their ears, and scratch their noses. what's this all about? How are you able to control it beat a public space and do so on time to react appropriately?

You can't do this. Too many details come to us too quickly, because excess chaff has been blended with wheat. you'll wonder if Janet is stroking her lip because she's worried about your idea? Alternatively, is she just rubbing an itchy chin quite often? On the opposite hand, you'll wonder if Jack will fold his arms since he resists your best efforts to vary direction for the entire cohort. Or is he just cold?

You can become insane by trying to intentionally track an area filled with people's constantly shifting body cues to little use because the discussion has transitioned on by the instant you figured it all out. within the meantime, you probably did not attend the discussion's useful content as you were alleged to.

Is there a route around this predicament of expecting to screen gigabytes of gushing information about some individuals' expectations, intentionally and quickly, while at the equivalence, considering the substance of the discussions?

You should know that it's possible. rather than checking the knowledge, for the foremost part, look for affirmation of your theories about expectation, in order that you'll accelerate and limit the flood of knowledge you've got to require in.

So, the real inquiry is this; if you would like to show into a conscious master in analyzing other individuals' oblivious articulation of their intentions, how would you structure speculations that articulation and affirm or dismiss them? the acceptable response is to confine your potential speculations to not many whom you've recognized before your gathering, discussion, or introduction. At that time, you'll suggest the only conversation starter to your intuitive personality and utilize that oblivious ability we, as an entire, got to give an unmistakable, solid answer.

So, we should always begin. Here are five, normal, helpful approaches to think about what other individuals mean:

The approaches are divided into:

- Open and closed
- Being sincere or insincere
- Being allied or opposed
- Strong and subservient
- Committed and uncommitted

You can, however, add yours, for specific circumstances not covered by these, and you'll find that each one these functions are within an outsized proportion of interactions between people where you would like to trace visual communication in particulars.

I'll touch every range. The aims are to spend a touch time that specializes in the nonverbal conversation at an upcoming meeting, and choose which continuum is best suited to what you're worried about or involved in, also to display the crux of the matter from you and therefore the folks that care.

Further, because the book addresses this, you'll be abandoning of all the control of your subconscious and, as if by magic, you will get an easy, accurate measure of what people want. It takes a touch procedure, but this may change the way you read others and enhance your ability to interact with them.

We will begin by examining a person's genuineness. How does one reveal the truth? Read on.

Sincerity Vs. Insincerity: together with your oblivious personality is that the most ideal approach to understanding the troubling inquiry of acknowledging a lie. Glance at the entire face and torso, and ask yourself whether it's sincere or not? Let's get right down to business at that level intuition. Perhaps the entire picture means a gentle articulation is basically great to grab. The face, for instance, is about during a smile but the eyes are cold? Dishonesty: are your eyes fixed with stupid stillness, as your hands interweave anxiously? That's an important symbol of being insincere.

The following most vital spot to see after the fact is that the direction of the top. Majority folks, once we lie, dismiss our head, tip it up or right down to move it far away from the opposite individual. that's the rationale you'd prefer to not concentrate tons on specific cues, but instead, let your conscious personality get on the overall situation. If you look tons at the eyes, for instance, you'll miss seeing that the top is turned down or sideways. So another time, ask yourself, is that this individual genuine or deceitful? And then, absorb the whole individual. you will have the choice to inform more often than not.

For those of you who are keen on the small print, you will need to understand some of the actual 'tells' in any case. aside from the eyes and face, look for the torso just in case they shy away from you, which can mean they're telling a lie, or toward you, which suggests they're telling the reality. Check whether there are guarded motions against the hands and arms and indications of tumult from the hands and fingers. Furthermore, look for opposing conduct from the legs and feet. If your partner says, "No, everything's fine," except his feet are situated unusually or his legs are clumsily crossed far away from you, those are signs to seem into his story further.

Likewise, tune for indications of strain within the voice. If you discover that the voice is painstakingly controlled or somewhat sharp sounding than expected, the individual could be endeavoring to disguise something. The world's best master of lying has discovered that individuals who are lying delay down with an end goal to regulate their voice, their facial expressions and different mannerism. In any case, even the standard individuals can likewise race to urge past a cumbersome inclination minute. So, the first concern to look for maybe a change of the voice from the norm, which you ought to know well, just in case of a spouse or a lover.

Recognizing a liar during a public gathering is an unprecedented exercise. Certain individuals have made a vocation out of recognizing small-scale articulations that hid fundamental feelings. In any case, it's an uncertain science because considerably more detail is absent, and you do not have a clue why the individual is covering the sensation. Is it dread? Anger? Energy? to urge that, you would like to become more familiar with the individual better, which requires a while investment.

Allied and Opposed

This category will assist you to note if someone is on your side or not.

How would you tell whether somebody is your ally or not? the elemental non-verbal communication to look for to make a decision if individuals are united to you or restricted is physical position and their direction. This makes for engaging people viewing. When you're on to the present a part of conduct, you will see that it's easy to urge.

Simply, individuals who are in understanding will generally mirror each other's conduct. One will lead, and therefore the other will follow. this is often particularly simple to inform when there are three individuals present, and you would like to form a sense of who is your ally and who isn't. look for the one that features a similar essential body direction as you. For a test, move and check whether the opposite individual sticks to the present same pattern within the following thirty seconds.

Companions, spouses, and darlings normally reflect each other's physical direction when they're at an equivalent place or with the general public and that they do inessential understand. It's fascinating to observe couples for indications of reflection and its inverse. you'll regularly recognize inconvenience within the relationship before the couple knows about it.

What occurs in reflection is more significant than simply understanding or associating. Since influence is enthusiastic even as a scholarly movement, it originates from deep inside the mind. At the purpose, once we concur with somebody, we do intrinsically with our entire being. you'll utilize this to drive understanding and make an influence. Embrace a stance, and watch others to receive it. once they have, they transform it somewhat. If the others come, you're well on your approach to convince the space.

The value of your power (or scarcity therein department), is going to be rendered and checked by your management of nonverbal communication within the hall. the reason is that the bodies of people reveal what they think, not the opposite way. It's both unreasonable and clear. Our brains state themselves fundamentally, I'm physically adapted with this woman, so I need to accept as true with her. That's because we do not like better to think we're behaving without reason.

You should utilize this control of the physical direction of other individuals with articulacy. It must be joined with a progression of steps that incorporate different types of agreement building. It won't work just to return into an area, receive a physical position, and expect every other person to embrace your scholar position also.

To start with, construct understanding by embracing their positions, managing their worries, and most significantly, expanding on your receptiveness to them and their receptiveness to you. do that work cautiously while you're talking through the problems critical to the circumstance. What you're doing is adjusting your two discussions and utilizing them to convince others within the room. It takes extensive practice to try to do this with nuance and viability, yet once you ace it, you will see that your capacity to convince others will increment immensely.

Strong and Subservient

In space and height, the story of power during a room is written. Scan the alpha. If possible, he or she would be the best person in the room. That's why kings and queens have had daises thrones since they started ruling others.

I did a test asking the CEOs, whom I worked with, to see the revelation of power out by convening a conference with the CEO within the Centre at a room table. The CEOs usually take the Centre of the space to demonstrate their power anyway, and sometimes even the top. Next, I advised the Chief executive to take a seat in her chair at the start, but after a short time, he progressively sinks into the chair by slipping very, very, gradually forward. Yes, to the conscious, yet invisible mind. the result was phenomenal. Those within the audience who were deliberately trying to articulate their subservience to the Boss sank right down to escape the boss upstage. The CEOs told me they might hardly suppress their laughter on hearing that everyone at the council table slide towards the ground

Powerful individuals also are taking over such a lot of space, splaying out their legs or arms, or hogging more room within the room. that's why influential people get larger apartments than fewer men, and that is why tall people in their careers are significantly more likely to rise faster than short people.

Powerful individuals use a number of bolder indicators of their dominance to enjoys shorter breaks, from upsetting smaller individuals to talking more. We make more or less eye contact due to their choice. In fact, they monitor the communication of the second speaker's ballet with the attention and therefore the outside contact. that's why it requires preparation to satisfy the Queen, and you've got to urge out of the space before you enter. All this is often just voicing her superiority over the remainder folks. Strong people may disappear from a discussion with this capacity, control speed, and show their power. I even have seen people leaning back during a meeting and putting their hands behind their heads to point out their dominance over the remainder of the gang. it's arrogant, but it's successful.

Non-verbal show capacity is all about regulating your behavior, also as others'. Once, it's something that's expertly tuned to by the subconscious; you'll immediately know when you're within the company for somebody who thinks she's strong due to all the signs I've mentioned, and you're all instinctively conscious of.

Committed and Uncommitted

Commitment is that the moment you shut the offer, the contract ink, get the work, get the 'go forward.' it's a key moment, and it is vital to be ready to see it in order that you wouldn't be doing the incorrect thing at the pivotal moment.

What is the texture of it?

People learn from you once they are serious. they're transparent, submissive sometimes, always genuine, and usually well connected. It starts with their eyes; they're completely open and you're focused. Likewise, the face is open. It's getting to be very on the brink of yours quite anything. It's all about completing the sale to shut the space. that's why car sales representatives regularly shake your hand. The torso, if not engaged, is accessible and nearer to you. From the arms and hands, feet and legs, there's no oppositional chatter. If appropriate within the situations, the person or persons could mimic you. The act of communication is usually indicated by a change of nonverbal communication, which suggests a choice has been made. look for it yes or no. Push your subconscious during a higher gear at that level. it's important to ask yourself if indeed the person is committed. You'll say easily once you see all of the positive effects I even have mentioned or the other. With time and in particular, you're getting to feel relaxed. The commitment may be a logical statement, and that we wish to achieve it because we are social creatures. The commitment may be a quite link that creates people feel good. once you function from your subconscious, you'll recognize once you see it. When there's no such thing, people have expressed their frustration with all types of anger, discordant visual communication, and efforts to quit. a couple of cultural norms spread these weird moments with an abundance of understanding, positive nonverbal communication, and shallow endeavors at duty. At the purpose when Westerners initially work from Asia, as an example, they often finish up misunderstanding the Asian act of kindness and need to hide it as a touch of eager to commit. this is often one occurrence when your consciousness can fail you. The examinations showed that the elemental non-verbal communication is initially the equivalent round the globe. However, it can rapidly be secured with socially decided non-verbal communication minutes later. Without plenty of coaching, the distinctions are often difficult to identify.

This isn't the spot for an all-inclusive exchange of various cultures, yet there are various phenomenal references regarding the matter. It's ideal to require societies individually, when you are going to go to another nation, as against attempting to find out them at an equivalent time. Exactly, because the non-verbal communication we convey is profoundly adapted by our childhood, and it's difficult to vary when it's not natural.

Open and Closed

The very first thanks to determining the motives of others, is that the most vital one; their level of transparency. it's the foremost important since interaction will start if people are honest with each other. Nothing good can happen if they are not. You need to be prepared to scale individuals more along the lines quite easily in an almost automated way with just a touch training. Nevertheless, don't invite an instantaneous reading, what people call thin-slicing lately. actually, it takes a touch time for every new individual you meet to live the performance of conduct. the thought isn't to be capable of completing this role immediately, but to be ready to take stock somebody with high efficiency in terms of whether this person is hospitable you or not, within a couple of minutes.

Past the forehead, see the flexibility of the eyebrows. How regularly and much do they move? Generally, individuals will cause the movement of their eyebrows when they're communicating with others, checking out a reaction, posing an inquiry, taking you in, etc. So, the sum and separation of movement are markers of a general degree of receptiveness, and on a specific occasion, when the eyebrows are up, being hospitable your contribution to the occasion. Once more, the event could be due to an inquiry that the individual has posed to you, yet it's considered being open.

Presently go right down to the eyes themselves. Is it true that they're limited or all the way open? you've got to line up a pattern of how the individual carries on in genuinely nonpartisan circumstances. Doing this may offer you an idea of whether the precise case is that of transparency or not. Individuals open their eyes more extensively once they are keen on an individual or thing, and shut them once they aren't, or are effectively suspicious or careful about occasions, individuals, or activities.

Since individuals are so dynamic with their eyes, you ought to be mindful to preclude ecological reasons. maybe a brilliant light sparkling within the individual's face? which will represent the lean eyes. it's going to not be because you've recently offered the individual a trade-in vehicle at an outstanding cost. If you'll, take an in-depth check out the pupils. How open or shut would they assert they are? Being open may be a representation of getting interest, fascination, and excitement; the inverse shows the turnaround. Moreover, the overall degree of lighting within the earth influences the dimensions of the pupils, so you've got to create up a typical ability to notice the difference.

Flaring nostrils are the results of romance books and novels about steeds. By the by, there could be truth to the portrayals associating sexual appreciation for this piece of the face, particularly if pheromones are being researched on and fascination finishes up being valid.

It is unquestionably things that a wrinkled nose can show disgust, or in any event, nauseate at an awful stench. Outrageous facial motions like these are difficult to miss and effectively delivered to the conscious mind. it's the subtler ones you need to be increasingly worried about. When somebody arrives at the aim of wrinkling his nose, they need presumably already revealed to you ways they feel or are getting to do intrinsically.

The mouth is fit thousand minor departures from the essential entourage of a smile, scowl, shock, dread, etc. In basic terms, look for a real smile. that's the widely comprehended indication of endorsement from others, and consequently, individuals who grin are sure to be available to you than impartial individuals. Individuals can have a smile due to different reasons; Note that it's essential to possess the wisdom to acknowledge a firm, troubled, or false smile from an off-the-cuff, regular one that's inviting and open.

Moreover, for the torso, proximity and bearing sign degrees of transparency. On a really basic level, the closer and every one the more direct location of the opposite person's torso toward you, the more open that individual is, and therefore the more distance they keep from you, the more closed they're.

What are those things hand gestures inform us concerning transparency? they're not the undeniable ones just like the harmony signal, or the middle finger. Those are referred to as 'symbols'. No, those we all make once we talk — the unimportant backup to discourse, as we wave our hands to believe a word or underline some extent.

These motions signal purpose constantly. At the purpose when individuals reach toward us with open motions, as an example, they're typically flagging transparency. Just occasionally are some things different, almost like one side snare to the jaw. A grasp, definitive open signal, maybe a blend of open hand motions and open torso.

Receptiveness is often perused within the hand itself too. what's happening with it? Is it gripped or apprehensively manipulating the opposite hand? Is it skittish or endeavoring to disguise itself during a pocket? Hands talk a perpetual and captivating language; they're glorious little weathervanes to the condition of the spirit inside and its purposes. On the off chance that you simply make an act of watching other individuals' hands, you will find out about the condition of their nerves, retentiveness, certainty, indignation, satisfaction, distress, advantage, or fatigue, notwithstanding, their transparency or deficiency therein department.

Numerous books on non-verbal communication imply to offer explicit implications of explicit motions, however, this is often a trick's down. Each signal can have an outsized number of implications. We fold our arms, to select a basic model since we're cautious, undoubted, though we're wiped out, cold, or we'd like to shroud a growing midsection.

However, if you're checking out the response to a specific inquiry, at that time you'll give your oblivious ability something to try to for you. Ask yourself, is that this individual open or shut toward me? Then start checking out the pieces of data that you simply need to make an assurance.

The ideal approach to try to do this is often to supply the conversation starter to your intuitive personality first. Solicit yourself toward the beginning from the discussion, open or shut? What's more, stay for your instinct about the difficulty, to show bent be clear. once you have a sense of the circumstance, you'll begin searching deliberately for pieces of data to affirm or invalidate your underlying reading.

Assume you're at a prospective employee meet-up, as an example, and you would like to acknowledge what your odds of accomplishment are. the first inquiry you ought to consider is whether or not you're even within the running or not. because it was, is that this a real meeting or a courtesy meeting? So, start the meeting asking yourself, is that this individual open or shut to me? If the acceptable response returns shut, at that time you'll be sensibly certain that another person as of now has the activity.

If the individual appears to be open, you'll activate your vitality and appeal. you would possibly get to be watchful for an adjustment therein reading. Consider the likelihood that the questioner has been open for; maybe the initial forty-five minutes of the meeting and afterwards all of a sudden begins to convey shut sign. it's going to be a perfect opportunity to vary strategies or cut the meeting off.

Has the questioner decided within the negative, or would she say she is simply flagging that the time is up? you would possibly get to ask some particular procedure inquiries (so anyone can hear and understand) to ascertain. for instance, "What's the subsequent stage? In what capacity will you approach deciding on a choice?" is that the inquiry to pose to your oblivious personality open or shut? On the off chance that the acceptable response is given during a shut manner, you presumably won't land the position. On the off chance that the non-verbal communication by then is open, you're still within the running. A bolder inquiry therein equivalent circumstance could also be to ask, "how would I stack facing different candidates?" Beset up for both a solution you wish and therefore the one you dislike!

Since grown-ups become adroit in controlling their countenances and chest areas, it merits taking a gander at the legs and feet for the fascinating counter flag. Frequently, somebody has made their face in an enjoyable welcome, yet the legs and feet (and the center as well) may recount to an alternate story. The legs could be crossed faraway from you, flagging a shut direction, the center could be contorted away, or the opposite individual may essentially expand the separation, even marginally, among you.

Decoding visual communication by Watching at the Body Movement

Understanding people could also be a tough thing to try to, but once you are doing it, you'll have conquered your way into their life, hence ready to influence them in various ways. during this book, we specialize in the positive manipulation which will work for your benefit. As we start this chapter, allow us to check out a number of the ways in which can assist you to understand other people's visual communication. subsequent time you're around your friends, during a work meeting, or with kids, just search for the subsequent and understand what they mean.

Arms and Legs Crossed Suggests Opposition to Your Ideas

Legs and arms crossed are obstructions that indicate that the opposite individual isn't receptive to what you tell. you discover that, albeit they have a tendency to interact within the good conversation and smile, most of the time the reality is revealed through visual communication. Authors who were doing negotiations for his or her new book on reading visual communication study a case. They held many meetings and later revealed that among all the meetings, not one resulted in an agreement whenever one among the parties crossed their legs and feet when negotiating. Mentally, the legs and arms crossed means a private is being mentally, emotionally, or physically stopped from what's before them. it isn't deliberate, so it is so surprising.

Copying Your visual communication

Have any of you ever met somebody and located that they are doing an equivalent if you cross or uncross your legs and feet? or even when you're thinking, they lean their heads the exact same position as yours? actually, that's an honest indication. If we experience a bond with another person, mirroring visual communication comes in unintentionally. It's a sign that the discussion is moving tolerably and your message is being received by that group. Such information is often particularly helpful when bargaining because it tells you what the opposite party feels about the contract.

The Story is Told by Posture

Have you ever seen someone inherit an area, and you immediately knew that they're in control? This influence is primarily about the language of the body, and sometimes involves an upright stance, movements with the palms facing forward, and usually open and expressive gestures. The brain is programmed to balance energy with the number of individuals taking over space. it is a position of authority to face straight together with your shoulders back; it seems to maximize the quantity of storage you fill. On the opposite hand, slouching is that the product of the collapse of your shape; it seems to require up less space and fewer energy for activities. Maintaining good posture commands respect and fosters commitment, no matter being during a leadership position or not.

The Eyes are Crinkled by Genuine Smiles

The mouth can deceive whenever it applies to laugh, however, the eyes can never lie. Genuine smiles touch the ears and crinkle the skin ahead of them to create the feet of the crow. Sometimes, individuals smile to hide what they could feel and think, so await crinkles at the sides of their eyes subsequent time you would like to understand if somebody's smile is real. If they are not there, something covers the smile.

Lying Eyes

The overwhelming majority folks presumably grew up hearing, "Look at me without flinching once you converse with me!" Our folks were working under the supposition that it's hard to take care of eye contact with someone when you're deceiving them, and that they were correct at some point. In any case, it's such basic information that individuals will frequently and purposely hold eye-to-eye connection trying to hide the way they're lying. the difficulty is that an outsized number of them overcompensate and hold eye-to-eye connection to the purpose that it feels awkward. All things being equal, Americans hold eye-to-eye connection for seven to 10 seconds, but longer when we're tuning in than when we're talking. just in case you're conversing with somebody whose gaze is making you squirm, particularly when they're extremely still and unblinking, something goes on and that they could also be lying you.

Discomfort in Raised Eyebrows

The three fundamental feelings that cause your eyebrows to travel up are shock, stress, and trepidation. Have a go at causing a stare when you're having an off-the-cuff easygoing discussion with a companion. It's difficult to try to, would I say it isn't? If someone who is conversing with you happens to possess raised eyebrows, yet the topic of the discussion isn't one that might consistently cause shock, stress, or dread, then there's something different happening.

Misrepresented Nods Signal Nervousness About Acceptance

At the purpose when you're telling somebody something and that they keep nodding an excessive amount of, this suggests they're stressed over what you think about them or that you simply question their capacity to stick to your guidelines.

A Held Jaw Sign Pressure

A gripped jaw, a hard and fast neck, or wrinkled temples are altogether indications of stress. Despite what the individual is stating, they're indications of serious inconvenience. The discussion could also be diving into something they're jittery about or their psyche maybe elsewhere and they are concentrating on what is wrong with them. The key's to seem for that befuddlement between what the individual says and what their strained non-verbal communication is letting you recognize.

Chapter 14. Interpreting Behavior Common Patterns

Common Patterns of Interpreting Behavior – Legs and Feet

When engaging in a conversation, we typically don't pay attention to the movements of the lower body. Since our direct line of sight is from the chest up, we often miss the obvious signs of the legs and feet. Certain stances that occur within the legs can signify dominance, sexual attraction, and even anxiety. Let's consider a few common patterns to look for when attempting to analyze someone else.

Crossed Legs

Crossed legs could indicate defensiveness. Perhaps you are sitting in a meeting at work, and your colleague says something totally off-putting. You may find yourself slowly crossing your legs as a subliminal way of showing your disapproval. Defensiveness could be heightened when one hand is positioned on top of the crossed leg. This is almost like a taunting move, signaling combat.

Crossing the ankles or knees are signs of nervousness, anxiety, and fear. This stance is protective in nature, which indicates that someone is attempting to protect themselves from whatever source of fear they are encountering. It could also be a means to control actions during high adrenaline situations.

Pointing and Active Legs

If you are miserable at a party, likely your legs are pointed towards the door as you are ready to leave. Our legs inadvertently point to where our heart wants to go. This can be used to determine interest and attraction. The legs, even when covered, will almost always point in the direction they are interested in.

Legs that bounce continuously could mean two things: boredom and nervousness. When you witness a person continuously bouncing their legs up and down, they may be nervous about something. This bounce is like a protective blanket that distracts their mind from their jitters. In addition, when someone is growing restless and ready to go, they may move their legs rapidly. The bouncing or tapping of the legs can be likened to a compulsion carried out to make the irritation subside.

When both legs point in one direction, it could be a clear indicator of interest for the person. However, when one leg steps back, it could indicate that the person wants distance. They may be uncomfortable with the person, conversation, or situation at hand. This subtle movement could be their way of escaping something distressful.

Messages from the Thighs

The upper portions of the legs usually indicate sexual or suggestive invitations between men and women. In daily activities, men may sit with their thighs opened as a sign of dominance. This outward display of masculinity represents an "alpha male" mentality. With women, closed thighs are a polite sign of femininity. Many young girls are instructed to sit with their legs closed so as not to expose their private areas. This closed manner of sitting is graceful and emanates class. When opened, they express dominance and even a form of female rebellion. Since it is so common for girls to be taught to keep their legs closed, doing the opposite could indicate opposition to societal norms. In addition, it is also extremely flirtatious to sit with the thighs crossed and one sitting higher above the other. This could indicate interest.

The feet work very closely with the legs to determine areas of interest. When the toes are pointed at a specific object or direction, this indicates where we want to go. This could be a subtle signal your body sends to your mind about certain situations. The feet are used to make a statement and could also be used as an accent to verbal cues. Stomping, imaginative kicking, or tapping are all means of gaining attention.

When toddlers throw tantrums, it's not only their flailing arms, crying eyes, and yelling demands that occur. Toddlers utilize their legs and feet to create loud noises to further emphasize their anger.

Much like moving the legs, bouncing the feet or excessive pacing are signs of anxiety. During moments of high adrenaline, the feet can be seen moving uncontrollably, almost like rabbit's feet. Signs of nervousness are also present when the feet are curled behind an object, perhaps the legs of a

chair or a table. Since curving the body inward is a subtle sign of inner protection, the feet follow suit with this protective stance.

Professor Geoffrey Beattie of the University of Manchester reveals that subtle foot movements and positioning could reveal signs of personality traits. He explains, "The weird thing about feet is that most people know what they are doing with their facial expressions; they may or may not know what they are doing with their hands, but unless we specifically think about it, we know nothing about what we are doing with our feet." Through his studies, he found that individuals with rather arrogant or haughty personalities typically kept their feet still as they were always aware of the self; whereas, shy individuals frequently shuffled their feet when sitting. This gives us insight into the characteristics of a person. Typically, shy people indicate high levels of nervousness or anxiety during social occasions. This directly proves the notion that foot movement equals anxiety. The beauty behind interpreting subtle body movements is that you can always find a glimmer of proof to solidify the theory.

Feet are also directly related to laughter. When we are extremely tickled by something, our feet come slightly off the ground. We may even partner that laughter with a slap of the knee. Dr. Beattie mentioned that men and women subconsciously show their attraction by combining feet movement during laughter. This indicates that the woman is comfortable enough with you to make obvious movements. As far as men, he says, "With men, feet aren't so important.

When it comes to interpreting the signs of the legs and feet, direction and movement are the two primary components needed for translation. Although we typically fret from glancing at the bottom half of a person, simple movements could be a key indicator as to how a person is feeling. It's imperative to understand the beauty of intricate movements in order to fully understand the inner workings of another person.

Common Patterns of Interpreting Behavior - Arms and Hands

A great deal of our emotions are expressed through our arms and hands. The warm embrace of a touch indicates love while a sharp slap translates to anger. Much of our productivity depends on the accuracy of our arms and hands when completing tasks. The movements of the arms and hands are quite obvious as they are used as a complement to verbal expression. Let's consider a few subliminal signals we receive from analyzing the hands and arms.

As our arms expand, we typically appear larger than our normal demeanor. This could be used as a descriptive means to explain how massive a person or object is, or this could be a subtle sign of instigating aggression or dominance.

It also indicates spatial awareness. A person could expand the arms to give the subtle signal that they prefer space. It could be likened to "marking their territory." On the contrary, when the arms expand but curve towards the person, this is reminiscent of a hug. This embrace indicates safety or protection. Many mother figures are seen welcoming their children in this manner.

Since we primarily use our hands and arms to gesture, they are extremely descriptive tools that express our emotions. When the arms are raised, this is a sign of frustration and overwhelming doubt. We can almost envision an overwhelmed person clenching their hands over their ears or on top of the head as a means of protection.

The crossing of the arms is a true indicator of how a person is feeling. When the arms are crossed, this typically means anxiety, shyness, fear, or disbelief. We can picture a frustrated mother or father crossing their arms towards their child when they do something naughty. However, when the arms are tightly crossed with the hands either balled into fists or nestled in the armpits, this signals combat. This occurs when an individual has been taunted. Their anger is essentially holding their arms inward as a protective means. The hidden fists could signal the person holding themselves back from doing something they would regret.

Individuals who have been exposed to violence or who feel vulnerable may have a strong dislike for people speaking to them with their hands in their faces. Even a slight gesture could signal a fight or flight response. When the arms are thrusting forward, this is a scare tactic usually intended to create emphasis. We fight with our arms and hands, so the connection between the two is threatening.

When the arms are positioned behind the backs and out of sight of the person they are engaging with, this indicates hidden intent. The person may lack confidence, or they are attempting to hide their fear through fiddling with their hands behind their backs. This isn't necessarily a sign of a liar. Rather, the person may simply feel uncomfortable, or they are preventing themselves from saying something.

The elbows, when facing out, could be a silent cry for space. A person may want others to back away from them without having to actually verbally express their disposition. This can easily be observed through the actions of children. Toddlers, who cannot communicate verbally, will often extend their elbows in a sharp motion in order to indicate space. As adults, we do this subconsciously as a means of inner protection.

The hands are quite detailed in their means of communication. One move of the hand can indicate an invitation while another movement could ignite conflict. When the hands are crossed with the thumbs tucked under, this is a signal of peace. East Indian gurus can be seen holding their hands in this way to express giving, peaceful natures. They wish to extend this light to others through their physical movements. When the hands are placed in front of the belly button, with the fingers touching and open palms, this is a symbol of dignity. The person is trying to show their partner that they are confident, professional, and conscientious.

The hands are also key indicators of direction. We use our fingers to point towards areas of interest. When the hands are placed delicately on the knees with the palms down, this could indicate submission, especially when leaning towards the opposite person. Women usually engage in this stance while attempting to show interest in a flirtatious manner. Hand gestures can also indicate movement. When the palm is facing a person, this translates to dismissal and disapproval. The person is using their hands to physically block the other person from their sight.

When the hands are touching parts of the face, this could translate to brainstorming, boredom, or even decision making. When the palms are essentially holding the face and cheeks upward, this is a clear indicator of a person attempting to wake themselves up from a boring situation. It shows disinterest in the most obvious of ways. However, when the index finger is pointing towards certain areas of the face, a person could be deep in thought. The positioning of the fingers as well as the firmness of their grasp is telling.

Excessive shaking that permeates throughout the palms and into the fingers occurs during high stress situations. A person may be so nervous, their hands begin to shake uncontrollably. This also is a sign of intense hunger. The hands and fingers begin to grow unsteady, thus displaying the body's lack of food. Slight trembles can also occur when a person is being caught in a lie or confronted for a mistake. They may be so angry that the shakes are their way of expressing that anger.

We use our hands to describe the size and stature of certain things. Much like the arms, they are used to accentuate the gravity of a story, describe the weightiness of a subject, and even demonstrate movement. They are our primary way of gesturing, and they can add great excitement to a story or a conversation. When working together with the arms, the hands can be a great indicator of a person's confidence. Touching creates a sense of warmth and community that connects people together. When analyzed carefully, the movement of the hands and arms can tell us key clues about a person's disposition.

Chapter 15.Eye Movement

Reading eye contact is important to understand the true status of an individual, even where verbal communication seeks to hide it. As advised, body language should be read as a group, we will focus on individual aspects of body language and make the reader understand how to read that particular type of body language.

Your pupils dilate when you are focused and interested in someone you are having a conversation with, or the object we are looking at or using. The pupils will contract when one is transiting from one topic to another. We have no control over the working of pupils. When one is speaking about a less interesting topic, the pupils will contract.

Effective eye contact is critical when communicating with a person. Eye contact implies that one looks but does not stare. Persistent eye contact will make the recipient feel intimidated or judged. In Western cultures, regular eye contact is desired, but it should not be overly persistent. If one offers constant eye contact, then it is seen as an attempt to intimidate or judge, which makes the recipient of the eye contact uncomfortable. There are studies that suggest that most children fall victim to attacks by pet dogs if they make too much eye contact, as this causes them to feel threatened and react defensively and instinctually.

Winking

In Western culture, winking is considered as a form of flirting which should be done to people we are in good terms with. This varies, though, as Asian cultures frown on winking as a facial expression.

Blinking

In most cases, blinking is instinctive; our affection for the person we are speaking to causes us to subconsciously blink faster. If the average rate of blinking is 6 to 10 times per minute, then it can indicate that one is drawn to the person they are speaking to.

Eye Direction

The direction of the eyes tells us about how an individual is feeling. When someone is thinking, they tend to look to their left as they are recalling or reminiscing. An individual that is thinking tends to look to their right when thinking creatively, but it can also be interpreted as a sign that one is lying. For left-handed people, the eye directions will be reversed.

Avoiding Eye Contact

When we do not make eye contact with someone we are speaking to for extended periods of time, we are most likely uncomfortable with the person or the conversation. We avoid looking someone in the eye if we feel ashamed to be communicating at them. When we feel dishonest about trying to deceive people, we avoid looking at them. While it is okay to blink or drop eye contact temporarily, people that consistently shun making eye contact are likely to be feeling uneasy with the message or the person they are communicating with. For emphasis, staring at someone will make them drop eye contact due to feeling intimidated. Evasive eye contact happens where one deliberately avoids making eye contact.

Crying

Human beings cry due to feeling uncontrollable pain or in an attempt to attract sympathy from others. Crying is considered an intense emotion associated with grief or sadness though it can also denote extreme happiness known as tears of joy. When an individual forces tears to manipulate a situation, this is referred to as "crocodile tears." Typically, though, if one cries, then the individual is likely experiencing intense negative emotion.

Additionally, when one is interested in what you are speaking, he or she will make eye contact often. The eye contact on the eyes of the other person is for the duration of 2-3 minutes, and then it switches to the lips or nose, and then returns to the eyes. For a brief moment, the person initiating eye contact will look down then back up to the eyes. Looking up and to the right demonstrates dismissal and boredom. Dilation of the pupil may indicate that someone is interested or that the room is brighter.

In some instances, sustained eye contact may be a signal that you want to speak to the person or that you are interested in the person sexually. At one point, you have noticed a hard stare from a man towards a particular woman to the point the woman notices and asks the man what is all that for. In this case, eye contact is not being used to intimidate but to single out the target person. You probably have seen a woman ask why is that man staring at me then she proceeds to mind her business but on taking another look at the direction of the man the stare is still there. In this manner, eye contact is used to single out an individual and make them aware that one is having sexual feelings towards the person.

However, people are aware of the impact of body language and will seek to portray the expected body language. For instance, an individual that is lying is likely to make deliberate eye contact frequently to sound believable. At one point, you knew you were lying but went ahead to make eye contact. You probably have watched movies where one of the spouses is lying but makes believable eye contact with others. The reason for this faked body language is because the person is aware of the link between making eye contact and speaking the truth.

Like verbal language, body language and in particular eye contact can be highly contextual. For instance, an individual may wink to indicate that he or she agrees with the quality of the product being presented or that he or she agrees with the plan. Eye contact in these settings can be used as a coded language for a group of people. At one point, one of your classmates may have used a wink to indicate that the teacher is coming or to indicate that the secret you have been guarding is now out.

Activity

1.   Go through your laptop or movie collection and skip to instances where acouple or lovers are quarreling and pay attention to their eye contact. Where possible, pick a movie or TV series that you are yet to watch and scan through until where there is a scene of a couple or lovers quarreling and pay attention to their eye contact.

For instance, pick any episode of the Game of Thrones and find any instance where people are quarreling or arguing. They need not be love scenes. Pay attention to their eye contact and try to summarize their eye contact and any other aspect of eye contact as nonverbal communication. What did you conclude from the eye contact of the select characters?

2.   If you are certain that your lover can handle it, try initiating a falseaccusation that he or she is planning to move out of the country and then act the part. While in the discussion or quarrel, try to pay attention to eye contact with your lover and discover what you can conclude. For this exercise, the topic should only be "trying to move out of the country" and no other topic. You should not introduce any other topic. At the end of the exercise debrief the lover by making them understand that it was a prank and a

learning experience of body language and proceed to make them know the role of body language.

3.   Try observing children especially when they cry. Do you think eachcrying episode of a child is genuine? Why or why not? How did you arrive at this conclusion? Have you felt manipulated by tears of a child or another person?

4.   Assuming that you have a robust relationship with your friends orclassmates, try staring hard at one of your classmates especially the opposite sex. When he or she looks the other way, do not drop your stare. What was the eventual reaction of the person you were staring at?

The eye can be described both as a "window to the world" and as a

"window to the soul," that is, to intrapsychic processes. The latter

processes, however, are closely related to the private thinking processes and emotional processes of man. Therefore, information about this in our context should not be discussed in detail. We do not want to operate or approach telepathy, but outward-looking better understand the signals that are constantly being transmitted. Therefore, we will pay more attention to these signals, or only to those interior-facing people who want to take on the environment or a current non-recording desire.

The Definite, Firm, Open View

Many people believe that a definite, fixed gaze should go hand in hand with an immobile pupil, as opposed to the "restless" gaze. But that's not true, because a "fixed" view is always an "unsteady" one. Think about it: If you remember the last time you looked really hard into someone's eyes (remember it?) ... you looked that person in the eyes, not in the eye. That is, your gaze kept moving from one eye to the other! If your last such experience was so long ago that you cannot imagine this process at the moment, go to the mirror and try "eye contact" with yourself!

Stop.

Do you have a clear picture of this process in your mind's eye? Then you understand that a firm look must be a moving one! If one were to really see someone else firmly in the eye (i.e. to fix him), then the feeling that was triggered by it would be a most alienating one.

Therefore, it is not surprising that one feels uncomfortable in the presence of some people who have "learned" and trained eye contact in an exaggerated form. If you for example, if you have the opportunity to speak with members of the Church of Scientology (also known as Dianetics), which is also in Germany, then you can watch this constant stare. If this is then accompanied by a frozen light "smile," as "masters" of the system understand it to "radiate," then the impression of having to deal with a robotic-programmed, depersonalized "person" becomes even stronger. Similar observations can also be made with American graduates of several "est courses," as well as with the followers of many juvenile sects, also with participants of some so-called rhetoric seminars!

Let us, therefore, hold that a "steady" gaze is also more alive. As all life pulsates, so does the pupil constantly to (fractions of a) millimeter (s) back and forth.

Eye Contact

As a rule, I would like to put the following sentence in the room:

Eye contact is called eye contact because it creates contact.

Now, eye contact can also avoid this contact, although he seems to be looking for him. This is the case when one stares at someone (as in the examples above). A rule of some rhetoric and communication coach states. For example, one should see the other firmly and definitely on the root of the nose. This cannot promote genuine, warm, understanding contact, but must be strange! In addition, the pupil movements when stared at a spot are so minimal that they can hardly be perceived by the naked eye. While a lively look, in which one "wanders" from pupil to pupil, is the kind of gaze we mean by eye contact!

Now the theory says that the eye is an excellent indicator of interest. But please do not forget that it can only be an indicator because also the chest cavity, as well as the mouth, play an essential role here.

In eye contact, we can, therefore, assume that the communication is "good." But what about when eye contact is avoided? First an experiment again: Have a conversation with someone in the near future, in which you will tell each other something. If you could quickly chat with a neighbor or colleague before you read on, it would be optimal. They will pay attention to eye contact and try to determine what "good" eye contact is.

Stop.

If you had the opportunity to try this, you may have already noticed the following statement:

Contrary to popular belief, "good" eye contact is not constant. Instead, we understand by "good" eye contact that the listener (almost) constantly looks at the, while the speaker looks at the listener less frequently. This is related to the fact that we cannot simultaneously think intensely and perceive information that is irrelevant to this process of thought. Therefore, a reflection often looks up at the ceiling (as if it were written there) or sideways away or down. This look is not really a look, because he is not consciously aware right now. He "looks inward," or "sinks in thought." The more someone has to think or want what he wants to say, the more likely he is to interrupt eye contact! You can also test this again specifically.

Eye Contact Experiment

Ask a person a question that you can expect to see have to think about it. For example, what did you do the day before yesterday? Or: When were you last in the cinema? Or: Can you spell "Nuremberg" backward? Here, you will find that most people in your introduction look away while thinking and beginning to speak. Only at the last words (or after that), the person looks back to you.

On the other hand, like every listener who maintains good eye contact, you have looked at your counterpart all the time so that your counterpart with small control glances can always catch your attention!

Two More Experiments!

Try to think about each statement for about ten minutes in a conversation before you announce it! You will notice that this seems impossible!

Then ask other people to try the same and talk about the difficulties you experience.

As a second experiment, you can try the following: a person who is speaking to you Over the shoulder of! You will notice that the speaker registers this out of the corner of his eye, even if he did not look directly at you. He will pause, maybe even look around, to see what has drawn your attention!

That is, although we often look away as we think, we can pick up a lot of signals out of the corner of our eyes or when we are sensitive. But there are also people who do not notice this, so they continue to talk "stubbornly," no matter what signals their environment is trying to desperately send them if they do not want to interrupt directly.

These two experiments will both increase your receptivity and be of great value in relation to what has been said below.

Eye Contact as A Strategy?

Although I strongly advise against the idea of "eye contact"

To use "strategy" as this will inevitably lead to excesses as described in 5.4.1, I would like to refer to the following rule:

Eye contact in the sense of control views represents an essential aspect of successful interviewing.

The emphasis is on "one essential aspect." On the one hand, the description of the experiment you have shown a possibility that includes the brief control view. On the other hand, it is a fact that one often looks away while thinking.

This brings us to a sin in negotiations, which unfortunately happens all too often:

Do you remember our party talk example; in which you were interested in the car of your counterpart? If we want to look at this situation as an example of a negotiation, then an important indication was his suddenly changing posture! After quoting the price we can pay for, he suddenly turned to us (shifting his body weight abruptly), claiming "far too little." Now imagine that you had to think about your price offer. Then you might have looked at the ceiling and calculated what the car, according to his explanation, includes everything. You might have thought, "He says the tires are new, a stereo is included ...." Imagine, you would have made your price offer still without eye contact. Then it would have been possible for him to sit back again until you looked again. That means you have the most important clue for your Price strategy!

People who are shy, or who seem to avoid eye contact. Here we often react wrongly by asking ourselves to feel uncomfortable and look away as well. Think about it: If you cannot look at the others for any reason, then this does not automatically mean that you do not want to be seen! If you look at him, of course not stare "firmly," possibly with a hint of a frown!), then his small, occasionally used control glances will show him that he is not "overlooked," disregarded, not taken seriously, etc.

Incidentally, I am always asked this point in the seminar: "Yes, but what about a counterpart who squints or stutters or is somehow crippled?" Answer: The cross-eyed person already has enough problems if squinting (as is often the case) is accompanied by a (partial) obstruction of vision. Why should we punish him? by preventing that he can be viewed? In addition, a person suffers with something affliction is mainly due to the fact that his fellow human beings never let him forget that he is "different" or "handicapped"! Our tendency to look away here is out of our own discomfort, not because we want to "help" the other, as verbally gladly claimed.

As for a man who stutters: Without going into the psychoanalytic and other theories offered here, we can say globally that most stutterers do not have a physiological defect that this way of speaking enforces. So, there is only the possibility of a "psychological" reason. Whatever this may look like (the theories differ here), the effect that is achieved is always the same: the stuttering human being forces his environment to pay more attention to him than a non-stuttering one. You have to concentrate more to understand it.

Incidentally, the same also applies to extremely quiet or unclearly speaking (e.g. mumbling) fellow human beings!

At first, the seminar participants claim that it makes people nervous when they look at them. But that's not true! Rather, it is true that these people are nervous (rightly), if you constantly look on the Mouth, what many listeners do automatically and unconsciously! You too would become nervous if someone constantly sees you on the mouth! Like everyone else, with whom you want to try this once! But that does not mean that we cannot look this person in the eye or should! It is this signal of eye contact that will improve your contact with someone, not avoiding it because you are embarrassed!

Pupil Size as A Signal?

As people have observed, a person whose pupil is contracted acts differently on us than someone whose pupil is wide open. The former view is called piercing. It is said of someone that he had "pig's eye" and so on. The latter is often perceived as an "open eye," though the eyelid itself may not really be very open. Short-sighted people have "beautiful" eyes, as the pupil is larger in order to compensate for the poorer vision. From this, it follows already that an extremely well-sighted person may, therefore, have a rather "piercing" look. Furthermore, it must be remembered that the lighting conditions absolutely must remain the same, if you want to interpret current pupil dilations as interest, or constrictions as disinterest! In addition, we generally have too little "feeling" for how large a pupil "right now" should be in order to be able to periodically evaluate pupil size as signals from time to time. "Lethich" could be a constriction

(If all the conditions of observation have been fulfilled!) Although this means disinterest, but: We have seen that a person who wants to "process" the information just heard, "sinks into thought," which process also coincides with a narrowing of the pupil accompanied! It's as if he meant to say, "For the moment, please no more Data, before I could think about the given. "This process indicates strong interest, because if not so acute interest he could us continue to talk without sending "shielding" signals of any kind.

From this, we can see how "exact" information is as follows: "Ask your partner if he loves you and pay attention to his answer to the size of his pupil."

The Eye Muscles

As already indicated, there are two parts of the eye, which we can observe: On the one hand the pupil, on the other hand, the total or movements of the eyelids.

So, one speaks from the "imposed" eye, when the upper lid is lowered. This view is accompanied by a limitation of perception. It may be temporary (a fraction of a second) or longer (several minutes). Again, many authors interpret "disinterest" here.

Even more shielding than the "imposed" effect is the "hidden" eye, in which the upper lid is almost closed. Even with "squinted" eyes, we obscure the sensory organ with which we see, for in mistrust, in reflection, in aggression; at moments when we do not want to see much! However, what we have said now for forehead wrinkling applies even more to the eye: there are always several muscles moving in association with each other. Eyelid movements are associated with both eyebrow movements (forehead area), as well as movements of the mouth muscles! Therefore, the rule that one should learn, the register primary signals of the eyes with these secondary features, the former conscious, the latter simultaneously, but unconsciously.

Ask someone to tell you something. His presentation should take a little longer, so several minutes. Questions like "How was it on vacation?" Or stories about a movie you're watching are great. Now the person has been asked for the information so that it (unconsciously) starts from the assumption that one will look at it during (attentive) listening. But you do not do that! Even if the person himself hardly looks at you because they are thinking, they will notice in small checks that there is no eye contact. This feels like an incongruent signal from us! Immediately, she will interrupt or ask, " what is?" Or something similar. Now assure "Keep talking." In hindsight, the person is usually unsettled or upset (rightly so).

So please do not exaggerate!

Nevertheless, such attempts train our eyes enormously, since we determined to induce signals deliberately and not to wait for seeing-practicing until they Eventually come up at random!

Although we have already filled pages with the review of the gaze, we have not yet discussed a fraction of the possible information. But here too it applies that less is more. If you learn to pay attention to the mentioned aspects, then you as a student already see much more than before!

Technically, the midface also includes the nose, as well as the cheek area (and of course the ears). But since the mimic possibilities of nose and ears are minimal, we will not address them here separately. The same applies to the cheek area, although I would like to point out that a relaxed person in the cheek area works differently than a tense one!

As the last information note:

You cannot relax the eye area as long as the mouth is cramped, and vice versa!

Chapter 16.Facial Expressions

Take into account your looks on the outside. Think about how much a person can pass on with just an external appearance. A smile may reflect happiness or approval. A fake smile can flag unhappiness or hopelessness. Our physical appearance can now and again show our specific feelings about a particular situation. While you're pretending you're feeling fine the whole phrase could tell people something else. Some examples of emotions that can be conveyed through physical actions include: Joy

- gloomy
- Getting angry
- Shocked
- Disgusting feeling
- Anxiety
- Feeling confused
- Happiness

Aspiration

Contempt

The attitude on the face of an individual may even help to determine if we trust or support what the individual says. One review showed that a minor trigger of a stir and a slight smile included the most consistent outward appearance. This articulation, as suggested by the specialists, transmits both friendliness and confidence. Physical appearance is also among the most diverse non-verbal communication styles. Comparable throughout the world are the articulations used to pass on fear, anger, resentment, and happiness.

A Scientist went on and found help for the completeness of a number of outward appearances linked to individual emotions, including euphoria, anger, fear, pain, and sadness. A study even suggests that we use their appearances and articulations to make decisions regarding the current knowledge of individuals. One study found that people with smaller faces and increasingly visible noses were expected to be deemed astute. Individuals with smiling, serene resonance were also selected to be more positive than those with articulations of frustration. Physical attributes do the share of a lion's responsibility in transmitting data to the next man. A regular person will not be able to explore the legs or arms' non-verbal communication. However, almost everyone can see the sign shown on an individual's heart. It is therefore of great importance that we maintain a reasonable and sufficient outward presentation in the event that we are abhorred by everyone because we are not receptive. The key articulation that everyone in a person is looking for is the smile. A smile can recover, but it can be difficult at the same time. A lady with a stiff-lipped smile that does not show any teeth is emblematic of her lack of enthusiasm for the debate, although it may seem to a normal individual that she is charmed by the continuous conversation.

Real and Fake Smile

There are numerous attributes of a unique grin. At whatever point individual grins normally, with no deliberate power, wrinkles are made around the eyes. This is because in a unique and real smile, the corners of the lip are pulled up and the muscles around the eyes are contracted. In a phony grin, just lip developments occur. Individuals giving phony grins grin just through their mouth and not eyes. Imagine a scenario where the individual who you are conversing with attempts to deliver a phony grin by wrinkling their eyes willfully. There is a stunt to distinguish this too. At the point when a grin is veritable, the plump piece of the eye between the eyebrow and the eyelid moves descending and the parts of the bargains additionally plunge to a slight degree. Research has demonstrated that the more individual grins, the more positive response he/she gets from the others. There is one all the more method to identify false grins. At the point when an individual attempt to counterfeit a grin, the right side of the hemisphere of the cerebrum – the one work in outward appearances sends flag just to one side of the body. Henceforth, a phony grin will consistently be more grounded on one side and more fragile on the opposite side. Be that as it may, in a certified grin, the two pieces of the cerebrum send signals and thus, the grin is similarly solid on both sides. If by any chance individual's eyes are turning away from you, at that point you should understand that the individual is exhausted from you and it is smarter to either change the subject of dialog or leave. Be that as it may, if the lips are marginally squeezed, the eyebrows are raised and there is a watchful eye of eyes at you alongside the head erect or somewhat pushed forward, at that point this suggests enthusiasm of the individual in you.

Eyes

Eyes have such an enormous significance in any discussion or association that if the language of the eyes turns out badly, the whole discussion and the notoriety of the individual turns out badly. Eyes communicate in a language that is inevitable from others' eyes. Eye to eye connection manages discussion and clues about accommodation and strength also. What individuals see about another when they meet just because are the eyes. Also, subsequently, both the gatherings included make speedy decisions about one another dependent on the eyes. Eyes are thus, the vehicle of passing on data about other individuals' frames of mind and contemplations. Give us a chance to take a gander at a portion of the messages passed on by the eyes.

The Dilating and Contracting of Pupils

At the point when somebody gets energized, the students get expanded and can widen up to multiple times the first size. On the other hand, when an individual is furious or in some other negative state of mind, the understudies contract. Thus, if you find that the other individual's students have enlarged, it implies the individual is keen on you or in your discussion. In any case, if the understudies have contracted, at that point, it is smarter to comprehend that the individual isn't intrigued.

The Flash of the Eyebrow

In pretty much every culture, a long separation "hi" is passed on by the brisk ascent and fall of the eyebrow. This is called as the eyebrow streak or flash. The brief instant development of the eyebrow is a method for welcome one another. In any case, in Japan, it has a contrary undertone and thus, must not be utilized with individuals from Japan.

The Eyebrows Game

The rise of your eyebrows during discussion suggests accommodation. Then again, the bringing down of eyebrows connotes predominance. Those individuals who deliberately cause a rise in their eyebrows are found to seem compliant and the individuals who lower their eyebrows are commonly viewed as forceful.

There is one trick here. At the point when women bring down their eyelids and cause a rise in their eyebrows simultaneously, it passes on sexual accommodation. This articulation must, henceforth, be kept away from informal and professional workplaces.

It is constantly prescribed that an individual must keep in touch with the other individual to show a degree of intrigue and expectation. Be that as it may, if you continue taking a gander at the other individual for quite a while, it might put the other individual at some inconvenience. The other individual might be threatened by your look. In many societies, it has been discovered that to construct a decent affinity with the other individual, your look must meet the other individual's look for about 60% to 70% of the time. If you continue looking at them with intrigue, different individuals will feel that you like them and subsequently, they will respond with their look also. In any case, if you find that the other individual isn't taking a look at you for a specific timeframe and is somewhat turning away from you constantly, at that point the discussion needs to end or the subject of the discussion needs to change. If you are uncertain of to what extent you should take a glance at the other individual, the most secure wager is to take a look at the other individual for the time the person is taking a look at you. Turning away during a cross-examination likewise gives away the signal that the individual is lying.

The Sideways Glance

The sideways look can be seen as a declaration of intrigue or even threatening vibe. At the point when a sideways look is joined with a grin or somewhat caused a commotion, it can convey intrigue and is additionally an acclaimed romance sign. Notwithstanding, if the sideways look is joined with a grimace, downturned eyebrows, and downturned lips, it can pass on doubt, analysis, or even antagonistic vibe.

The Blinking Magic

The rate at which your eyes squint is additionally a transport of important data. If you are keen on somebody or somebody's discussion, you won't flutter your eyelid as frequently. Be that as it may, on the off chance that you are not inspired by somebody, your pace of squinting the eyes will increment drastically. Increment in the squinting pace of the eyes passes on a lack of engagement or fatigue.

The Dart

If the eyes of the other individual start to shoot from one side to the next, it suggests that the individual has lost enthusiasm for you and is searching for break courses to be away from you. This uncovers the other individual's instability.

The Authority Gaze

One approach to radiate authority is to bring down your eyebrows, slender the eyelids and spotlight intently on the other individual. This gives an impression of what predators do right before assaulting their prey. The flickering rate needs to diminish and there must be a consistent spotlight on the other individual's eyes.

Eye to eye connection and eye developments are a significant piece of our relational abilities and furthermore our non-verbal communication. Thus, it is of most extreme significance to keep in touch with the other individual, without threatening that person. Eye to eye connection assumes a critical job in deals interviews, prospective employee meetings, and easygoing discussions too.

Fingers

Regardless of whether the eyes, arms, and legs are at a legitimate spot, the fingers can in any case play as a spoiler. The hands and the fingers together give away a great deal of data about us and different individuals too. Besides, when we talk with our hand signals and finger developments, it is simpler for the other individual to hold what we have spoken about. Thus, hand developments help in the maintenance of messages as well. Give us a chance to investigate the distinctive hand motions that are regularly seen in the world over.

Scouring of Palms

The scouring of palms against one another is seen to be an indication of hope. Scouring of palms together is representative of having the desire for positive results. This articulation is very regular in deals pitch also. The business groups of numerous associations advise about an idea to other individuals utilizing collapsed hands and palms scouring against one another.

Scouring the palms at a quicker rate shows that the individual is thinking about the advantages for the other and is an amicable individual. On the other hand, a moderate rub of hands with a grin passes on that the aims are insidious and the individual is narrow-minded.

Thumb and Finger Rub

The scouring of fingers and the thumb against one another shows that the individual has a hope of getting cash. This is one motivation behind why this signal must be utilized with an alert before individuals.

Grasped Hands

Individuals who stand or sit with grasped clench hands pass on dissatisfaction. Individuals embrace grasped clench hands when they are on edge, furious or tired of something, yet are attempting to control themselves. The grasped clench hands can hide the antagonistic sentiments of the individual when the individual is losing some arrangement or isn't liking his present involvement.

The Steeple

The steeple is the motion which an individual given by putting his fingers of one hand over the fingers of the other hand and shaping a congregation steeple. This signal shows certainty and can likewise radiate position, and as a rule, prevalence. This motion should be maintained a strategic distance from on the off chance that you need to convince somebody, as it can give an off-base sign that you are attempting to be haughty and are attempting to force your contemplations as opposed to attempting to persuade.

Face Platter

The face platter is a positive body gesture where an individual, particularly a woman, puts the fingers of one hand over those of the other and afterward puts her jawline on the mix of fingers. This is utilized to build one's allure and is an approach to display one's face to the next.

Clasping Hands Back

Clasping hands back is an approach to show prevalence, power, and certainty, and is regularly embraced by illustrious families, police power, or the military. Alongside a straight back and jaw held up, it shows that the individual holds authority and merits stunningness and regard. This stance is prescribed to those individuals who feel strained during prospective employee interviews.

If one hand holds the wrist of the other hand, it passes on dissatisfaction and an endeavor of restraint. As the hand climbs the other hand from the wrist, the degree of dissatisfaction being radiated increments. If an individual holds his arm with the other hand, it implies that the dissatisfaction level of the individual is high.

One additionally should be mindful of the presentation of thumb out in the open. If your thumb distends out of your petticoat or your pocket, it is representative of forceful demeanor and predominance. This signal is generally embraced by individuals of high social stature.

If an individual has placed their hands inside the back pockets and the thumbs are projecting, at that point, it shows that the individual is attempting to conceal some inclination from us. A few people close their arms but then, continue showing their thumbs. That is once more, an approach to show predominance alongside indicating that he/she is shut to discussions.

Revealing Lies Through Body Language

In this universe of consistently developing duplicity and falsehoods, it is critical to know when an individual is lying. Getting untruths isn't that a troublesome errand given you recognize what you have to search for to spot liars.

Taking swallows and covering one's mouth doesn't show that the individual is lying. In any case, it shows that some data is being covered up. A liar consistently needs harmoniousness in his outward appearances. At the point when an individual lie, the subliminal piece of the cerebrum conveys an apprehensive sign that shows up as non-verbal cue, in this way repudiating what the individual has recently been talking. Numerous individuals scratch their nose or jerk their ears or even rub their nose. Numerous multiple times, a brief instant jeer shows up on one side of an individual's face, indicating that the individual is lying or is being mocked about what he is talking about. It has additionally been seen that appealing individuals are found as more truthful in public forums and subsequently, numerous multiple times, alluring individuals can get off with lies without being recognized or addressed by any stretch of the imagination.

Now, let us discuss the most common lying non-verbal cues that you can watch out for

A Covered Mouth

This is for the most part seen in kids. The individual covers their mouth while talking an untruth. It is an automatic demonstration of preventing tricky words from leaving the mouth. The mouth can be secured utilizing a couple of fingers, utilizing the palm(s) or in any event, utilizing a clench hand. A few people likewise attempt to mask this demonstration by giving a phony hack. This additionally shows the individual is attempting to hide some data.

The Nose Touch

Liars are for the most part found to give a fast touch to their nose while lying. It very well may be a couple of hurried rubs or even an ambiguous pinch of the nose. This signal must be perused alongside different motions being referenced here. Some of the time, individuals experiencing cold and hack can likewise similarly contact their nose and subsequently, must not be regarded as liars.

The Nose Itch

While lying, the body discharges synthetic substances called catecholamines, which cause the tissues inside the nose to grow. The expanded circulatory strain makes the nose to grow and causes the nerve endings inside the nose to shiver, in this manner makes it bothersome. Subsequently, when an individual tells something false, the individual feels an expanded need to fulfill the tingle by consistently stroking the nose.

Scratching the Neck

Liars tend to scratch at their necks also. It is not a genuine tingle in the neck as a real tingle will require some huge number of rubs on the neck. In any case, liars simply scratch their necks around four to multiple times and they will in general repeat it commonly.

Getting the Ears

Liars additionally feel some sort of shivering in the ears. Research has discovered that liars feel an increased propensity to scratch their ears when they are lying.

Scouring the Eyes

At the point when an individual has some untruths, the person will in general turn away from the individual being deceived. Along these lines, the liar feels an inclination to rub one's eye to obstruct seeing the other individual. This is again one of the demonstrations that give a clue to the individual being a liar.

Chapter 17.MicroExpressions

A microexpression is an ultrafast display of a particular emotion that flashes across someone's face. It is so quick that an untrained observer is usually unable to catch it. Even the person who exhibited the microexpression is unaware that they did it. The seven universal microexpressions are contempt, disgust, happiness, surprise, anger, sadness, and fear. These expressions are so primal that they are expressed the same across people no matter where on earth they were raised. An Inuit person's microexpressions will look identical to those of an American person or a Japanese person's or a Haitian person's.

Reading Microexpressions

Knowing the best way to read and understand microexpressions is important because it helps you read a person's nonverbal actions. Here is a short guide on understanding microexpressions.

Happiness, contempt, fear, surprise, disgust, sadness, and anger are the seven universal microexpressions. These can happen very quickly. Looking at a person's face is the best way to know how somebody is feeling. The bad news is that most of these are usually overlooked. The show Lie to Me was based on Dr. Paul Ekman's research. He has conducted numerous studies on how to decode facial expressions. He has proven that all facial expressions are universal.

This just means that people who live in the United States will make the exact facial expressions as people who live in Madagascar who hasn't ever seen a movie or television show. People who were born blind are going to make the exact same expressions even though they have never seen anybody's face. Ekman designated seven expressions that are used most often and are easy to understand. Figuring out how to read them can be helpful when trying to understand other people. If you would like to practice reading faces, you need to know the basic expressions. It would be a good idea to practice these facial expressions in a mirror so you can see what they look like. You may even realize that if you make the expression successfully, you might actually feel that same emotion. While facial expressions can cause emotions; emotions actually cause facial expressions.

Happiness

- The corners of your lips will be drawn up and back.
- Your mouth might or might not be parted with your teeth exposed.

There will be a wrinkle that runs from the outer nose to the outer lip.

Your cheeks will be raised.

Your lower eyelid might be tense or showing wrinkles.

There will be some crow's feet on the outer corners of the eyes.

Contempt / Hate

There will be one side of the mouth raised.

Fear

- Your eyebrows will be drawn and raised together most specifically in a straight line.
- Wrinkles on the forehead will be in the center between the eyebrows and not all the way across.
- Your upper eyelid will be raised but the lower is drawn up and tense.
- Your eyes will have the white on the top half showing only. The lower whites won't be showing at all.
- Your mouth will be open with the lips drawn back, tensed, and stretched.

Surprise

- Your eyebrows will be raised and curved.
- The skin beneath your brow will be tightly stretched.
- Horizontal wrinkles go across your forehead.
- Your eyelids will be open with the whites show above and below. Your jaw will be slack, teeth apart, but there shouldn't be any tensions or stretching of the mouth.

Disgust

- Your upper eyelid will be raised.
- Your lower lip will be raised.
- Your nose will be wrinkled.
-
-

Your cheeks will be raised.

There will be lines that show just under your lower eyelid.

You make this expression when you smell anything horrible. **Sadness**

- The inner corners of your eyebrows will be drawn in and up. The skin beneath the eyebrows will be triangulated. The inner corner will be up.

- The corners of your lips will be pulled downward.

- Your jaw will come up.

- Your lower lip will stick out a bit.

This is the expression that is the hardest to fake.

Anger

- Your eyebrows will be lowered and drawn together.

- You will have vertical lines between your eyebrows.

- Your lower lid will be tense.

- Your eyes will be bulging or in a hard stare.

- Your lips could be pressed together firmly, with the corners drawn down, or shaped like a square like you are shouting.

- Your nostrils might be dilated.

- Your lower jaw will jut out.

- All three areas of the face have to be engaged not to have any ambiguity.

Once you have practiced these for a while, see if you can spot them in the people you are around the most.

Chapter 18.Touch

We engage in touching routinely. We commonly shake hands as greetings or assign to signal shared understanding. Touch as a form of communication is called haptics. For children, touch is a crucial aspect of their development. Children that do not get adequate touch have developmental issues. Touch helps babies cope with stress. At infancy, touch is the first sense that an infant responds to.

Functional Touch

At the workplace, touch is among effective means of communication, but it is necessary to keep it professional or casual. For instance, handshakes are often exchanged within a professional environment and can convey a trusting relationship between two people. Pay attention to the nonverbal cues that you are sending next time you shake someone's hand. Overall, one should always convey confidence when shaking another person's hand but you should avoid being overly-confident. Praise and encouragement are communicated by a firm pat on the back. Remember, people have varied reactions to touch as nonverbal communication. For instance, an innocent touch can make another person feel uncomfortable or frightened. Touch can become particularly complicated when touch is between a boss and a subordinate. Generally, those in power will utilize touch with subordinates to reinforce the hierarchy of the workplace. It is usually not acceptable for it to occur the other way around. For this reason, you should make sure to be careful even in the instance of using the most trivial of touches and resolve to enhance your communication techniques with your juniors. A standard measure is that it is better to fail but remain on the side of caution. Functional touch includes being physically examined by a doctor and being touch as a form of professional massage.

Social Touch

In the United States, a handshake is the most common way one engages in social touching. Handshakes vary from culture to culture, though. In some countries, kissing one or both cheeks is more common than a handshake. In the same interactions, men will allow a male stranger to touch them on their shoulders and arms whereas women feel comfortable being touched by a female stranger only on the arms. Men are likely to enjoy touch from a female stranger while women tend to feel uncomfortable with any touch by a male stranger. Equally important, men and women process touch differently which can create confusing and awkward situations. One should be respectful and cautious. For instance, while you stand close to a stranger on an elevator, it is not acceptable to stand so close to them that you make contact with him or her.

Friendship Touch

The types of touches allowed between friends vary depending on the context. For instance, women are more receptive touching female friends compared to their male counterparts. Touch is different depending on the closeness of the family and the sex of the family member. Displays of affection between friends are almost always appreciated and necessary, even if you are not a touchy person. One should be willing to get out of their comfort zone and offer their friend a hug when he or she is struggling.

Helping others enliven their moods is likely to uplift your moods as well.

Intimacy Touch

In romantic relationships, touches that communicate love play a critical role. For instance, the simplest of touches can convey a critical meaning such as holding hands or placing your arm around your partner which communicates that you are together. Adults place more emphasis on nonverbal cues compared to verbal cues when communicating according to recent studies on communication. In the earlier stages of dating, men tend to initiate physical contact in line with societal norms, but in later stages, it is women that initiate contact. Women place more premiums on touch compared to men and even the smallest of gestures can help calm women they were upset.

Arousal Touch

Arousing touches are elicited by intense feelings and are only acceptable when mutually agreed upon. Arousal touches are meant to evoke pleasure and can involve kissing, hugging, and flirtatious touching, and are often intended to suggest sex. One should be careful about their partner's needs. One can greatly improve their communication skills and relationships by considering the nonverbal messages you send via touching behavior.

Additionally, our sense of touch is intended to communicate clearly and quickly. Touch can elicit subconscious communication. For instance, you instantly pull away from your hand when touching something hot even before you consciously process. In this manner, touch constitutes one of the quickest ways to communicate. Touch as a form of nonverbal communication is an instinctive form of communication. In detail, touch conveys information instantly and causes a guttural reaction. Completely withholding touch will communicate the wrong messages without your realization.

Ways of Improving Touch in Appropriate Contexts

Pat someone on the back when you grant them praise.

If your colleague or friend has graduated, earned a promotion or married then pat them on the back. Giving a pat suggests that you are happy with the person and are encouraging them. Touch has a therapeutic value that relaxes the mind and the body as well as helping an individual feel secure and appreciated. At school, you must have felt valued and loved if you were patted on the back.

Initiate discussions with a touch to create cooperative relationships. Studies have established that touching a person increases their willingness to cooperate and work with others. Establishing physical contact with an individual that you wish to initiate a conversation with can help. Sometimes the target person may not realize that you touched them but will register subconsciously and establish a bond.

Extend the handshakes.

Shaking hands shows confidence and simplicity in interacting with others. Touch helps build trust between two people. Make your handshakes firm when shaking hands with people. It is also necessary to remember that some health conditions may make one shy away from shaking hands and this includes hyperhidrosis which makes the palms of the person sweat. With sweaty hands, the individual is likely to shun handshakes and this has little to do with the context of the conversation.

Adjust the touch type with respect to context.

As indicated, touch is highly contextual. For instance, the Japanese do not favor shaking hands and a person in this environment will avoid shaking hands at all costs. In the American context, shaking hands is encouraged. For this reason, one should adjust their touch type depending on the contexts. It might be welcome to hold the hands of your partner continuously while the same is creepy when talking to a stranger or to a colleague at the workplace.

Another form of touch is tickling which is mostly reserved for lovers, parents versus children, and peers. For instance, a mother may tickle her baby which is a therapeutic touch and is permissible. On the other hand, children or students of the same age set may tickle each other, which is permissible. However, it is inappropriate to tickle an adult when you are not lovers or the relationship between you and them is formal.

Touch as a form of abuse

Expectedly, there is a thin line between permissible touch and physical abuse. If not certain one should avoid initiating touch unless fully certain of its meaning to the target person. Pushing someone or pinching someone is considered a form of physical abuse. Kicking or striking someone as well as strangling are forms of physical abuse.

Touch as a game

In some contexts, a touch is a form of the game especially teasing. Touch as a form of the game should only happen where the participants are peers and are receptive to it. For instance, your friend or classmate may blindfold your eyes with the palms of their hands from behind. The participants in this tease may touch each other, for instance, the blinded person may try to feel your arms or head to try to guess the identity of the person teasing. In this form of touch, the scope of teaching allowed is large and may be equivalent to that of lovers.

Chapter 19: Spotting Romantic Interest

In this chapter, we are going to be taking a look at how to spot romantic interest through the analysis of body language, facial expressions, and other non-verbal clues. Also, we will be making gender-specific analyses as romantic interest varies greatly based on a person's gender.

Spotting romantic interest is one of the most popular topics of all time. Consistently, both men and women are interested in learning more about how they can determine if a person is genuinely attracted to them.

This topic is part science and part art. There is plenty of scientific evidence that backs up the reasoning behind attraction while there is an instinctive component, which cannot be adequately measured or quantified through scientific methods. What this implies is that if you are looking to gauge someone's level of attraction, then you need to have both a scientific approach and reliance on gut feelings.

To start things off, it should be noted that attraction works differently in men than it does in women. While the underlying biochemistry is essentially the same, the physical manifestations are different. In addition, cultural norms may govern romantic interactions to a varying degree.

For example, more conservative cultures frown upon any advances made by women while more liberal societies have a level playing field, that is, both men and women are free to pursue the object of their interest.

In that regard, it is worth mentioning that while many of the non-verbal clues are the same, women tend to be a lot more subtle than men are. In contrast, most men tend to be very open about their feelings toward the object of their attraction. While this shouldn't be taken as a blanket statement, it is a general rule of thumb. After all, there are plenty of shy men out there who have trouble making their interest known while there are plenty of women who are quite overt about their feelings for the object of their interest.

One other note with regard to attraction is that romantic interactions are generally perceived to be between men and women. Nevertheless, the nonverbal signs discussed in this chapter are perfectly applicable to same-sex relationships. After all, what matters is the person who is sending the signals and not necessarily the recipient.

That being said, I intend to have this discussion cover the entire spectrum of male and female interaction within a romantic context. That way, the information presented herein will provide you with the insights you need in order to improve your ability to pick up on the non-verbal clues indicating potential romantic interest and attraction.

Now, the first to keep in mind is that attraction is somewhat hard to define. The reason for this is that men and women seek different things in a potential mate. We are operating under the assumption that there is genuine attraction among those involved and not some hidden agenda spurring interest.

In that regard, the attraction is based on the qualities of an individual that meet or exceed the needs of the other. Hence, women tend to focus on different qualities in their potential romantic partner, whereas men tend to focus on a different set of qualities.

For instance, women tend to seek security and stability in a romantic partner. This is due to an instinctive need for survival and preservation of the species. In order to fully comprehend this, we would need to go all the way back to the day of primitive humans in which there was no guarantee that offspring would make it past their first year of life. As such, women, designated as a caregiver from the start, needed to secure the means and resources needed to ensure the survival of their offspring. On the other hand, the males were in charge of playing the role of provider.

In the early days of humankind, males were mainly hunter-gatherers. This means that they needed to go into the fray to find food. Whether food came from hunting or foraging, males were expected to provide the sustenance needed to ensure the survival of their offspring.

In contrast, males needed to find healthy females who had the physical qualities that would ensure their fertility and ability to bear children. I know that this sounds very primitive, but it is important to underscore this point as humans we are hardwired under this context. Consequently, thousands of years of evolution and biology are just now being challenged by the new social paradigm in which we find ourselves.

Over the last two hundred years or so, the dating paradigm has shifted dramatically.

Traditionally, most marriages were arranged. As such, it was not so much about love and romance, but about the position and financial stability. This paradigm lasted for a few centuries. Since the outset of the Industrial Revolution, the attitudes of society changed in such a way that men and women were free to choose who they wanted to marry. This opened the door for a number of circumstances.

So, men went from courting women to dating them. This meant that men needed to ensure that a woman would be willing to reciprocate his intentions and feelings. In contrast, women played a more passive role, and they were conditioned to wait for men to make the first move. However, they could drop subtle hints regarding their interest. That way, the man would be certain that he had a chance with a given woman.

In modern times, we are faced with a very liberal dating scene. While some countries have far more cultural and religious restrictions, most countries are fairly open about the manner in which they can pursue the object of their desire.

Consequently, it is imperative that both men and women gain deeper insight as to how attraction is expressed by either gender.

So, let us start off with men.

Men are a lot easier to read, as they tend to be far more overt about their interest in someone. They will generally seek the object of their interest and engage them in some manner. Typically, men will try to engage the other party by displays of strength, wealth, or status. These are signs that they are providers or protectors. In short, men try to position themselves as the best possible mate their object of interest can find.

Some general guidelines include direct eye contact, tilting their body toward the person they are attracted to and seeking constant physical contact. The latter generally tends to make most women uncomfortable, as unsolicited physical contact can get rather awkward quickly.

Other not so subtle hints that men drop are following the object of their affection around, placing their hands, or arms, as a sign of possession and frequent fidgeting. In fact, fidgeting is a dead giveaway as it is a sign that a man is nervous in the presence of whom they are attracted to.

In addition, some men might go silent (remember the freeze response?) and even fail to react in the presence of the object of the attraction. This reaction is partially due to the freeze response but it also due to the fact that some men freeze up when they don't know what to do or how to react.

This is why you see most dating advice that is oriented to men focus on what to do and what to say in various situations. What this does is that it eliminates a man's reliance on his wits by providing him with a set of tools. These tools are certainly useful though they may not be universally applicable.

One common method used by men is to approach and pull back. This method consists in approaching someone they are attracted to and then pulling away.

Then, they will engage and withdraw until they are able to make progress, say, go on a first date. The logic beneath this approach is that men tend to come on very strong when they are attracted to someone. As such, this approach allows them to find a balance between displaying their intentions and giving the object of their attraction some space.

As you can see, men are far more open about their attraction toward someone based on the permissiveness that society has afforded men throughout history. However, women have been traditionally tagged with a more submissive role. Therefore, women are not always able to express their intentions overtly in the same way that men do.

Some not so subtle signs of attraction in women are eye contact, hair pulling, and trailing off in conversation.

When a woman is attracted to a person, she will seek eye contact. This eye contact tends to be rather brief as women are not interested in winning a staring contest. They just want to signal to the object of their interest that they are willing to be engaged.

Another telltale sign of attraction in a woman is related to her hair. If you see a woman playing or pulling on her hair when speaking to someone they like, you can be pretty sure that she is indicating a willingness to be engaged.

Also, women who are interested in a person will allow for closer physical contact. Any a time a woman keeps people at arms' length, it is a clear indication that they have no interest in them. By the same token, any time a woman avoids eye contact and tilts their body away from the person they is interacting with, it is safe to assume they are not interested in being engaged.

Women are generally focused on faces. What this means is that when a woman is attracted to someone, they will not only focus on their eyes but also their mouth. They generally tend to watch the other party's lips when they speak. This is an instinctive reaction based on their desire to find a strong and healthy mate. Consequently, healthy-looking eyes, teeth, lips, and skin are clear indicators that a person is in good physical condition.

Women also drop many hints with their arms and hands. A woman who is uninterested will almost always cross her arms and/or legs at some point. If you find that a woman is sitting in the manner on a date, then the other party has a tough time ahead for them.

Conversely, if a woman is actually interested in the other person, she will sit, or stand, in a very "open" position, that is, hands at her sides (or folded on a table) and legs uncrossed. Also, leaning forward while listening to the interlocutor is a good indication that they are interested in what the other person has to say. If they make direct eye contact on various occasions, then the combination of clues is virtually a declaration of intent.

Some women refrain from eye contact when they are genuinely attracted to someone. They may cross gazes but quickly look away or perhaps look down. In some cultures, this is the norm, as it is a sign of submission. Western cultures don't normally have such customs though women may still prefer to avoid eye contact in order to prevent themselves from being too obvious.

Additionally, women will allow some type of physical contact as a sign of attraction. For instance, they may lightly brush their hand up against another person's or they may even give the object of their attraction a gentle tap on the shoulder or arm.

While this is, by no means, an invitation for further physical contact, it is a sign that a woman is comfortable and ready to take the interaction to a more personal level. This type of light touching can be reciprocated by similar touching.

Finally, a woman's voice says a lot about the way she feels. Women tend to speak with a higher pitch when they are in the presence of someone they are attracted to. Also, they may raise the tone of their voice in order to be "noticed" by the person they are attracted to. In one on one interaction, don't be surprised if you see a woman speaking somewhat faster. However, if she begins to slow down, then that might very well be a signal that she has lost interest.

On the whole, men and women will exhibit very similar signs of attraction such as open lips, rounded eyes, eyebrows higher than usual and the classic pupil dilation (this is actually very hard to spot). However, hands, arms and body positioning are far more indicative of attraction than other signs commonly mentioned.

In addition, facial gestures such as smiling are good indicators though not foolproof. After all, you might be talking with someone who is upbeat and positive. However, that does not mean that they are attracted to you.

In many ways, spotting attraction is a question of observation. So, pay close attention to the signals that you are receiving. They can help you to differentiate attraction from simple friendliness. That being said, you can also use these hints to indicate your own interest to someone.

In that regard, it is best for men to moderate their behaviors and mannerisms when interacting with someone they like. While it is certainly important to make their intentions known, it is also important to be more subtle. Being too open and direct can cause the other person to feel uncomfortable and even intimidated. Naturally, this will lead to an ineffective interaction.

So, for the men out there, dial it down a bit. You can send more subtle hints such as less direct eye contact and some light touching. For example, a handshake that lasts just a little longer than it should is a great way of signaling interest.

As an exercise for this chapter, I would recommend that you pay close attention to these signs when you are in restaurants, bars and other places where couple usually go on dates. Take the time to observe couples' interactions in order to identify the signals they are sending out. That way, you can get a good sense of knowing when someone is genuinely attracted, and when someone is not. Also, don't forget to take notes. These notes will help your thoughts on the right track.

Chapter 20: Spotting Insecurity

The indications of frailty point to the reality you never have a sense of safety. Unreliable individuals never have a sense of security, acknowledged, or OK. It incurs significant damage.

Few out of every odd uncertain individual gives indications of weakness the equivalent. What is frailty? It is actually what it implies. There will never be the point at which you have a sense of security, genuine, or secure in your very own skin. The most serious issue with being uncertain is that it doesn't generally seemed to be what it is. It is frequently misconstrued by the individuals around somebody uncertain.

Why? Since nobody needs to concede they live in dread of pretty much everything, that sounds insane. Thus, most uncertain individuals attempt to veil their nervousness, and spread it up with constant practices that don't work. They accomplish things that get them the careful inverse of what they hunger for— affection and acknowledgment.

indications of instability to watchout for

In the event that you wonder on the off chance that you are with somebody unreliable, or in the event that you ask whether you are uncertain yourself, these are the indications of instability that can't be covered up.

#1 They stress over everything. Did I say everything? I mean the world. There is definitely not a solitary thing that somebody who is unreliable doesn't stress over. They stress over their subsequent stage since they aren't sure they will arrive on safe ground. They consistently feel like the subsequent stage is sand trap.

#2 They never have a sense of security or settled. An uncertain individual never feels like they are protected or settled in their own life or in their very own skin. Normally encounters in their past sustain the frailty. They live in a condition of impermanent and they never get settled in light of the fact that it could all be no more.

#3 They pose similar inquiries again and again, as though they can't acknowledge the appropriate response. Like a youngster, they ask you similar inquiries again and again and over. How you answer matters not, they won't acknowledge your answer except if it is negative. They absolutely never put stock in anybody since they anticipate the most exceedingly awful.

#4 They push you away and afterward pull you back in. Somebody who is shaky needs to pull you in. At that point when you get excessively close, they monstrosity out and push you away. Their very own dread of dismissal drives them to continually push the very individuals they need close, far away. At that point once you leave, they implore you back.

#5 They continually inquire as to whether you are distraught or what they have done. Weakness prompts them always inquiring as to whether they have planned something for make you distraught. Stressed that they will lose you in the event that they don't do what you need and how you need it, their stressed nature has no base.

#6 They reliably apologize regardless of whether there's no expression of remorse essential. Never certain about themselves or how they run over, somebody shaky consistently feels as though they have accomplished something incorrectly and aren't above saying 'sorry' regardless of whether they haven't done anything by any stretch of the imagination.

Just so nobody is irate or angry with them, they simply express sorry to learn anything they could've done.

#7 They tend to disrupt their connections. Individuals who are uncertain never feel commendable enough to be seeing someone, causes a consistent uneasiness and dread that they will be discovered and left behind.

That prompts overcompensations to things and pushing individuals away when they dread that things are going gravely to ensure themselves. That can get them the very outcome they endeavor to evade in a relationship.

#8 They feel like everybody despises them. Perhaps the greatest indication of instability is that uncertain individuals always feel like everybody despises them. They can't generally disclose to you why or put their finger on what the issue is. They simply feel like everybody detests them.

#9 They stress in the event that somebody is speaking seriously about them constantly. Shaky individuals stress continually that individuals talk over them despite their good faith. Not having any desire to be disdained by individuals throughout their life, their instability drives them to persistently scan for affirmation that individuals don't care for them and are castigating them. For the most part, when there is no premise.

#10 They leave each circumstance thinking about whether they irritated anybody or aggravated somebody. Individuals who are unreliable are tension baffled practically constantly. They stress on the off chance that they said something rotten and replay the occasions of each snapshot of their social communications with individuals.

#11 They don't feel great in a gathering, so they for the most part have one individual they stick to. Uncertain individuals seem like outgoing people since they as a rule shroud the instability and turn on the appeal.

However, they ordinarily prefer to have one individual to stick to that makes them progressively secure and genuine. Typically just having the option to have each dear companion in turn, their kinship is their wellbeing zone when out with others.

#12 They strike hard when harmed. Uncertain individuals are continually injured. Their emotions are routinely harmed, which leads them to strike out against somebody who damages them. For the beneficiary, it appears to be an all out eruption.

Yet, because of the measure of strife and dread going on in the uncertain individual's psyche, it resembles repetitive sound never stops. Only one more thing in a flash sets them over the edge.

#13 They attempt to dazzle you, yet feel like a fraud inside, which makes them an apprehensive wreck. Most uncertain individuals don't appear to be shaky until you become more acquainted with them. Truly adept at veiling the individual so frightful inside, they build up a hard external shell, which makes them feel like a fraud constantly.

#14 Being distant from everyone else is their most exceedingly terrible dread. For unreliable individuals, being without anyone else is about the most noticeably terrible thing they can envision. They need other individuals to make themselves feel like everything is ok and safe. On the off chance that they lose somebody near them, it is overpowering, particularly somebody they love.

#15 They ache for endorsement, yet won't acknowledge it at any rate. Somebody uncertain pines for acknowledgment and endorsement. In any event, when given to them, they don't accept or acknowledge it. Regardless of whether the very thing they want gazes them in the face, they will not see it.

#16 They characterize themselves by what other individuals consider them. Uncertain individuals let other individuals disclose to them who and what they are on the grounds that they aren't very certain for themselves what they are made of. Always hoping to satisfy others and increase their acknowledgment, on the off chance that somebody doesn't care for them, it endures a colossal shot to their confidence.

#17 When you are with them you nearly feel the stirring of tension. Unreliable individuals are only difficult to be near. You can't put your finger on it, however they once in a while sit, they infrequently quit talking, or they simply have an anxious nervousness that tails them any place they go.

#18 They tend to be a fussbudget. Unreliable individuals don't have confidence in themselves, so they return and re-try everything around multiple times. Despite everything it won't ever be correct.

#19 They are envious of your associations with other individuals. Unreliable individuals are very tenacious. When they make you their stone, they get extremely desirous when you connect with another person.

They need you next to them to feel like nothing is wrong with the world and secure. In the event that you aren't bolstering their spirit, it feels vacant. They need 100% of you.

#20 They go overboard to apparently basic things. Since they continually convey a rucksack of apprehension, the littlest thing appears to set them off for reasons unknown.

Persistent uneasiness is a troublesome thing to live with and can have somebody hitting the verge out of the blue and now and again making a mountain out of a molehill.

Chapter 21: How to Control Your Body Language

Body language can enhance your communication skills in a great way. You can have effective communication skills, only if you can control your body language. Before, we look at the most used body language for manipulation. It is important to know how to take charge of your own body. Can we base these with the quote that, 'Charity begins at home?' Yeah, you cannot have an interest in understanding how to manipulate other people positively, yet you do not know how to take control of yourself. Let us kick off with understanding and having control of our body language.

How to Take Control and Manipulate Your Body Language

Research has shown that, when you are aware of the happenings of your own body, you can manipulate it by training yourself to have control, and even mold it to have effective communication. Further research recommends that you take some breathing exercises before going into a meeting or presentation. It will help you calm as well as have the ability to take note of your posture and gestures while on presentation. As you have noted by now, mirroring is a good technique. Always try to be keen on what the next person is doing non-verbally and copy that. It will help you become more effective in your communication with them. They will understand you better because this tunes your mind to the ability to communicate more truthfully at a place of relaxation.

However, you should be careful while shaping your body language. This is to ensure that the body language that you portray matches with what you are trying to present. A mismatch may bring confusion and may not be relevant at the moment. The person you are in conversation with my mistake you for meaning something else contrary to what you intended. The secret to having control of your body language is to take your time to learn it, to be aware of your non-verbal cues, as you apply what you learn.

The Body Language That Will Help You Take Charge of Your Space

Effective management involves individuals being able to encourage and have a positive influence. In planning for an important appointment maybe with your employees, management team, or partners you are focusing on what to say, memorizing critical points, and rehearsing your presentation to make you feel believable and persuasive. This is something you should be aware of, of course.

Here is what you should know if you want to take control of your position, at work, at a presentation or as a leader.

Seven Seconds is What You Have to Make an Impression

First impressions are essential in market relationships. When somebody psychologically marks you as, trustworthy, or skeptical, strong, or submissive, you will be seen through such a filter in any other dealings that you do or say. Your partners will look for the finest in you if they like you. They will suspect all of your deeds if they distrust you. While you can't stop people from having quick decisions, as a defense mechanism, the human mind is programmed in this way, you can learn how to make these choices effective for you. In much less than seven seconds, the initial perceptions are developed and strongly influenced by body language. Studies have found that nonverbal signals have more than four times the effect on the first impression you create than you speak. This is what you should know regarding making positive and lasting first impressions. Bear in mind several suggestions here:

Start by changing your attitude. People immediately pick up your mood. Have you noticed that you immediately get turned off after you find a customer service representative who has a negative attitude? You feel like leaving or request to be served by a different person. That is what will happen to you too if you have a bad attitude, which is highly noticeable. Think of the situation and make a deliberate decision about the mindset you want to represent before you meet a client, or join the meeting room for a company meeting, or step on the scene to make an analysis.

Smile. Smiling is a good sign that leaders are under using. A smile is a message, a gesture of recognition and acceptance. "I'm friendly and accessible," it says. Having a smile on your face will change the mood of your audience. If they had another perception of you, a smile can change that and make them relax.

Make contact with your eyes Looking at somebody's eyes conveys vitality and expresses interest and transparency. A nice way to help you make eye contact is to practice observing the eye color of everybody you encounter to enhance your eye contact. Overcome being shy and practice this great body language.

Lean in gently the body language that has you leaning forward, often expresses that you are actively participating and you are interested in the discussion. But be careful about the space of the other individual. This means staying about two ft away in most professional situations.

Shaking hands This will be the best way to develop a relationship It's the most successful as well. Research indicates that maintaining the very same degree of partnership you can get with a simple handshake takes a minimum of three hours of intense communication. You should ensure that you have palm-topalm touch and also that your hold is firm but not bone-crushing.

Look at your position. Studies have found that uniqueness of posture, presenting yourself in a way that exposes your openness and takes up space, generates a sense of control that creates changes in behavior in a subject independent of its specific rank or function in an organization. In fact, in three studies, it was repeatedly found that body position was more important than the hierarchical structure in making a person think, act, and be viewed more strongly.

- Building your credibility is dependent on how you align your non-verbal communication

Trust is developed by a perfect agreement between what is being said and the accompanying expressions. If your actions do not completely adhere to your spoken statement, people may consciously or unconsciously interpret dishonesty, confusion, or internal turmoil.

By the use of an electroencephalograph (EEG) device to calculate "eventrelated potentials"–brain waves that shape peaks and valleys to examine gesture effects proofs that one of these valleys happens when movements that dispute what is spoken are shown to subjects. This is the same dip in the brainwave that occurs when people listen to the language that does not make sense. And, in a rather reasonable way, they simply do not make sense if leaders say one thing and their behaviors point to something else. Each time your facial expressions do not suit your words e.g., losing eye contact or looking all over the room when trying to express candor, swaying back on the heels while thinking about the bright future of the company, or locking arms around the chest when announcing transparency. All this causes the verbal message to disappear.

- What your hands mean when you use them

Have you at any point seen that when individuals are energetic about what they're stating, their signals naturally turned out to be increasingly energized? Their hands and arms constantly move, accentuating focus and passing on eagerness.

You might not have known about this association previously, however you intuitively felt it. Research shows that an audience will in general view individuals who utilize a more prominent assortment of hand motions in a progressively ideal light. Studies likewise find that individuals who convey through dynamic motioning will, in general, be assessed as warm, pleasant, and vivacious, while the individuals who stay still or whose motions appear to be mechanical or "wooden" are viewed as legitimate, cold, and systematic.

That is one motivation behind why signals are so basic to a pioneer's viability and why getting them directly in an introduction associates so effectively with a group of people. You may have seen senior administrators commit little avoidable errors. At the point when pioneers don't utilize motions accurately on the off chance that they let their hands hang flaccidly to the side or fasten their hands before their bodies in the exemplary "fig leaf" position, it recommends they have no passionate interest in the issues or are not persuaded about the fact of the matter they're attempting to make.

To utilize signals adequately, pioneers should know about how those developments will in all probability be seen. Here are four basic hand motions and the messages behind them:

Concealed hands - Shrouded hands to make you look less reliable. This is one of the nonverbal signs that is profoundly imbued in our subliminal. Our precursors settled on endurance choices dependent on bits of visual data they grabbed from each other. In our ancient times, when somebody drew nearer with hands out of view, it was a sign of potential peril. Albeit today the risk of shrouded hands is more representative than genuine, our instilled mental inconvenience remains.

Blame game I've frequently observed officials utilize this signal in gatherings, arrangements, or meetings for accentuation or to show strength. The issue is that forceful blame dispensing can recommend that the pioneer is losing control of the circumstance and the signal bears a resemblance to parental reprimanding or play area harassing.

Eager gestures - There is an intriguing condition of the hand and arm development with vitality. If you need to extend more excitement and drive, you can do as such by expanded motioning. Then again, over-motioning (particularly when hands are raised over the shoulders) can cause you to seem whimsical, less trustworthy, and less incredible.

Laidback gestures Arms held at midsection tallness, and motions inside that level plane, help you - and the group of spectators - feel focused and formed. Arms at the midsection and bowed to a 45-degree point (joined by a position about shoulder-width wide) will likewise assist you with keeping grounded, empowered, and centered.

In this quick-paced, techno-charged time of email, writings, video chats, and video visits, one generally accepted fact remain: Face-to-confront is the most liked, gainful, and amazing correspondence medium. The more business pioneers convey electronically, all the more squeezing turns into the requirement for individual communication.

Here's the reason:

In face to face gatherings, our brain processes the nonstop course of nonverbal signs that we use as the reason for building trust and expert closeness. Eye to eye collaboration is data-rich. We translate what individuals state to us just halfway from the words they use. We get a large portion of the message (and the majority of the passionate subtlety behind the words) from vocal tone, pacing, outward appearances, and other nonverbal signs. What's more, we depend on prompt input on the quick reactions of others to assist us with checking how well our thoughts are being acknowledged.

So strong is the nonverbal connection between people that, when we are in certified affinity with somebody, we subliminally coordinate our body positions, developments, and even our breathing rhythms with theirs. Most intriguing, in up close and personal experiences the mind's "reflect neurons" impersonate practices, yet sensations and sentiments too. At the point when we are denied these relational prompts and are compelled to depend on the printed or verbally expressed word alone, the cerebrum battles and genuine correspondence endures.

Innovation can be a great facilitator of factual data, but meeting in an individual is the key to positive relationships between employees and clients. Whatever industry you work in, we're always in the business of individuals. However, tech-savvy you could be, face-to-face gatherings are by far the most successful way of capturing attendees ' interest, engaging them in a discussion, and fostering fruitful teamwork. It is said that if it doesn't matter that much, send an email. If it is crucial for the task, but not significant, make a phone call. If it is extremely important for the success of the project, it is advised to go see someone.

- Ability to study body language

More business administrators are learning how to send the correct sign, yet also how to understand them. The most significant thing in correspondence is hearing what isn't said."

Correspondence occurs more than two channels verbal and nonverbal bringing about two unmistakable discussions going on simultaneously. While verbal correspondence is significant, it's by all account not the only message being sent. Without the capacity to be able to read non-verbal communication, we miss critical components to discussions that can emphatically or adversely sway a business.

At the point when individuals aren't installed with an activity, pioneers should have the option to perceive what's going on and to react rapidly. That is the reason commitment and withdrawal are two of the most significant signs to screen in other individuals' non-verbal communication. Commitment practices demonstrate intrigue, receptivity, or understanding while separation practices signal fatigue, outrage, or protectiveness.

Active participation sign incorporates head gestures or tilts the widespread indication of "giving somebody your ear", and open-body poses. At the point when individuals are locked in, they will confront you straightforwardly, "pointing" at you with their entire body. Be that as it may, the moment they feel awkward, they may edge their chest area away – giving you "the brush off." And if they endure the whole gathering with the two arms and legs crossed, it's far-fetched you have their upfront investment.

Additionally, screen the measure of eye to eye connection you're getting. Generally, individuals will in general look longer and with more recurrence at individuals or things that they like. A large portion of us are alright with eye to eye connection enduring around three seconds, yet when we like or concur with somebody, we consequently increment the measure of time we investigate their eyes. Separation triggers the inverse: the measure of eye to eye connection diminishes, as we will in general turn away from things that trouble or get us bored.

Non-verbal communication is winding up some portion of an official's close to the home brand. Extraordinary pioneers sit, stand, walk, and signal in manners that ooze certainty, capability, and status. They additionally send non-verbal signs of warmth and sympathy, particularly when supporting community situations and overseeing change. As an official mentor, I've been awed by the effect that non-verbal communication has on administration results. Great nonverbal communication abilities can assist you with spurring direct reports, security with crowds, present thoughts with included believability, and truly venture your image of mystique. That is an incredible arrangement of aptitudes for any pioneer to create.

Detecting Lies through Voice & Language

Remember that the tone of a person's voice varies also from one to the other – hence the baseline. Once you've established the base, please watch out for the following changes since they're typical indicators of lying or hiding something.

Voice pitch

Studies suggest that derivations from the normal voice pitch can also indicate lies. An individual telling a lie could either have his voice pitch an octave higher or even lower.

A low voice pitch could indicate shame in the lie while a high voice pitch could easily indicate defensiveness in uttering the lie.

Large inhale

Inexperienced liars may perhaps 'strengthen' themselves through taking one deep breath before giving an answer. Also breathing may also become rapid or slow down as they do their best to calm the nervous tic.

Lip licking

Lying can also put a lot of stress to someone who's not used to lying. This can cause dry mouth, thus people who lie tend to also lick their lips more than usual.

Too casual

In some cases, a liar acts nonchalant – too nonchalant. They may even yawn, inspect their nails, & do anything to make everything seem normal.

If the person you're talking to doesn't usually act this way (baseline) then the deviation may perhaps be a way to hide the lie.

Hesitation & pauses

Although they can also be signs of anxiety & nervousness, hesitations & pauses are more indicative of lies & fabrications. Obviously, the person telling the lie is confused or just starting to concoct the lie in their minds, therefore causing lots of pauses & fillers such as 'umm' & 'hmmm'.

Conversation change

People who lie also prefer to have the conversation done quickly. If you think the person you're talking to is lying, just suddenly perform a quick change of topic.

A lot of liars will have no problem following with the change, some even relaxing at this quick switch in the conversation.

A truthful individual however would be a little confused while others may perhaps even question why you've changed the topic.

Word choices

Unconsciously, people who're telling a fib distance themselves from the actual story - as if they're watching what happened instead of doing the actual movements.

Word indicators include sudden drops in "me" & "I" storytelling. Note that this's a case to case basis.

Also pay attention to the context of what they're saying – a person lying would often switch their pronouns or even indicators since they're having a hard time following their own story.

Ask questions

Following the thought that on-the-spot-liars are making up the stories as they go, you can almost always easily catch someone by asking further questions about what they're saying.

This's a very common technique used by law enforcement in an effort to 'trip' the individual into revealing the truth.

One of the best ways to catch a liar would be by asking them to simply tell their story backwards, but do this subtly.

For example: so you jumped after the screech?
A lot of people memorize events in order. A person who's remembering an event has no problem talking about it backwards but someone who's simply 'creating' the memory will have a hard time with a reverse order. You can also ask them to retell the story backwards.

Those who've rehearsed their lies only do so in a progressive chronological manner. You can spot a liar if they're having difficulty in narrating their story backwards.

Observe their Answers

Liars have a hard time filling in the gaps – which's why it's common for them to   just 'repeat' what you say in answer to a question. For example: Q:
Did   •   you eat all the ice cream?
•
   A: No, I didn't eat all the ice cream

Also note the use of contractions. Contractions are often more natural & therefore more truthful: Q: Did you eat all the ice cream?

A: No, I <u>didn't.</u> (truth)

A: No, I <u>did not</u>. (lie)

Sarcasm

Some liars simply try not to answer a question directly, often resorting to sarcasm in an effort to distract you from the truth.

They may also imply an answer instead of giving a direct one.

Body Language – Most Common Indicators of Lies

Stillness

Lying takes its toll on people, especially mentally. This's why when a person is lying, they may become completely still – as if they're concentrating all their energy on creating the lie.

Distancing

When a person is distancing themselves from you, this can also actually indicate lying. The move isn't always so obvious.

In most cases, a person would simply lean their upper body backwards or even perhaps shift their feet so it isn't pointing directly towards you. In some cases, a very blunt step backward is just a dead giveaway.

Clenching

Clenching may actually occur in any body part – but it usually happens on the hands or the feet. Clenching is indicative of trying to reign in something, either anger or even sadness, or any other powerful emotion.

When lying, a clenching motion usually means that the liar is doing their best to establish some form of control. Excessive & unusual sweating is also part of lying because they're nervous that they might be caught.

Lower body

Individuals who're lying tend to shift their body away from their accuser.

However, this might not always be possible – so just observe the feet. Is their lower body slightly turned away from you?

This indicates that they want to leave the conversation & uncomfortable about what's going on, possibly due to the reason that they're lying.

Why're there opposing 'signs' to lying?

You're probably asking – why's it that 'fidgeting' is a sign of lying but 'stillness' is also one? Don't they contradict each other? You're absolutely right!

This's why the book placed emphasis on establishing a baseline first & foremost. It's essentially a comparison game.

What does this person do when telling the truth? If he stands still when answering a baseline question, then there's also all likelihood that he'll start to fidget when lying.

More than anything, reading body language & lies is a process of elimination – which's why reading someone you're close to is almost always easier.

What about practiced or planned lies?

If you'll notice, most of the indicators here apply for 'on the spot' lies. This's when individuals were forced to come up with the lie just a few minutes before it was said.

Individuals who planned the lie beforehand may've more vague signs. Hesitations, pauses, & eye shifting may disappear since they've 'created' the lie beforehand.

Don't worry though – a poker player always has a tell, which's why if you know the person well , there's a good chance that you can identify the actions that're off the baseline.

Practiced or planned lies can be hard to detect, but if you suspect that something's not right, you can quickly ask the person questions to verify what he or she just said.

Strip away a layer of their comfort by showing that what they're saying isn't clear to you.

Chapter 22: Mind Tricks To Gain A Better Rapport With People

Rapport & its significance

So what's Rapport & what's its significance in relation to the topic under discussion? Rapport can be described as a harmonious relationship that can be established between two parties so that they can simply feel comfortable in each other's presence, & be able to communicate better. Here again, we realize the importance of the subconscious mind. In order to build rapport with a particular person, we need to employ certain strategies that'll help us get in sync with that person. Building rapport is a crucial skill, critical for the resolution of sensitive problems. For example, carrying out negotiations in a hostage situation would require that you build a rapport. Without establishing a link with such people, there would perhaps be no way to resolve the situation. Without a good rapport, the safety of the hostages would become compromised which's a matter of serious concern. Although this example might seem a bit extreme, it demonstrates the need for rapport nicely. Even in our daily lives we need to be able to understand people better so that we can resolve conflicts & get people to agree with our goals.

Cues that you can use to your advantage

There're four basic cues that give us a lot of information regarding the mindset of a person & how they'll react to certain stimuli. We can use this information to tailor our demeanor in such a way that the other person feels comfortable in our presence. Getting them into their comfort zone will easily allow us to gauge people better. Only then will they reveal their true selves & intentions.

In order to build rapport we employ a technique called mirroring. This means to recognize the personality of the person you're speaking to, & then try to imitate those emotions, needs, or goals.

What do hand gestures reveal?

Hand gestures give us a lot of information about the personality of a person. Whenever you're immersed in conversation with a person, try & note what they're doing with their arms & hands. If you see that the person doesn't flail their hands around much when talking, try & refrain from doing much gesticulating yourself if you're looking to build rapport. You should also look at their body posture. If the concerned person is leaning forward, they're open & interested in what you've to say. Whereas if they're leaning back, it means that they're being protective, or closed off, & there might be a lack of trust between the two of you. Now is the time to adapt your strategy accordingly.

Since hands are very important, let's discuss a bit more about them.

Imagine that you're meeting someone for the first time. You shake their hand & you find their grip to be weak. You'll immediately think that this person is weak willed & that he's not very excited to see you. Hand gestures are some of the most important gestures & can often reveal a lot. In this chapter we'll go over some hand gestures & see what each of them can signify.

Openness & honesty:

If you're looking for signs of openness & honesty, look towards the palms. This's one of the most accurate ways of judging someone's intentions & deciding whether they're telling the truth or not. Have you ever seen a common gesture that people often use, they hold up their hands or extend them to you as they try to assure you about the total veracity of some claim. Now we've already established that a lot of people don't pay attention to their gestures so this falls under the heading of unconscious gestures. This can also give you a clue as to someone's real intentions. This gesture also originates from the childhood.

When children have done something wrong or when they're trying to hide some mischief, they hide their hands behind their back. Similarly, adults also follow the same techniques, albeit with more sophistication & subtlety. A cheating husband is likely to tuck his hands in his pockets or to cross his arms defensively as he proceeds to give various untrue explanations. This should also immediately signal to the other person that something's being hidden or that a lie is being told.

Intentional use of palms to deceive:

After reading the last paragraph, you're probably wondering that if you lie with an open palms gesture, would you be able to deceive people. The answer is probably not. Unless you're very practiced at the art, your consciously open palms won't be congruent with the rest of your body gestures. Hence, you may be caught out. It's possible, however, to make yourself appear more credible by practicing open palm gestures when communicating with others.

Palm power

Palm gestures are probably some of the most important & powerful of all gestures. If they're employed properly, they can give a person the power position in that particular interaction. There're three main manifestations of the gesture: palm up, palm down & the pointing finger with the palm closed gesture. Imagine that you asked someone to pick up a box & put it in the other room for you.

When you were relating this task, what was the actual position of your palms? How did you gesture towards the box & the room? Palm facing upwards is usually taken as a sign of submission & humility. It would mean that you're asking or requesting someone to do something for you. The palm facing downwards is seen as a sign of authority. It means that you're ordering the next person to do something. The pointed finger means that you're trying to beat the other person into submission. It's one of the most irritating gestures that you can make so it'll be a good practice to try & avoid this gesture as much as possible.

Shaking hands

You already know that shaking hands can easily give you powerful insights about the other person. One of the first things that you'll be able to pick up in a handshake is the direction of power in that particular relationship. You'll notice whether someone's trying to dominate you, being submissive or treating you equally. These attitudes are transmitted unconsciously, however with practice you can easily develop a dominant handshake. This's usually done by reaching with your palm facing downwards relative to the other person's hand.

Palm facing upwards usually transmits submission. When two dominant people shake hands, it's usually a power play as they both grip each other's hands, building rapport & respect. The result is a vice-like handshake with both the palms remaining in the vertical position.

If you want to neutralize someone's dominant handshake, just focus on your feet. This can be done by stepping with your left foot forward as you step into the other person's intimate zone. You should also practice doing this.

Although shaking someone's hand is a form of greeting, you should also first see whether it would be welcome or not. Never force a handshake on someone who doesn't want to shake hands with you.

Handshake styles

The palm-down thrust is certainly the most aggressive handshake style as it rarely gives the receiver little chance of establishing an equal relationship. There're some maneuvers to counter it. A simple one is to grasp the person's hand on top & then shake it. This puts you in the dominant position. However use it with caution as it also embarrasses the other person.

The glove handshake is also sometimes colloquially known as the politician's handshake. Effusive people often employ it. It's meant to relay the impression of trustworthiness & honesty, however it can come off as a sign of someone being fake, especially if it's used on a person recently met. It's also often taken to signify pretension & dishonesty. Hence, it should be used carefully & only on long time acquaintances.

Everyone dreads cold & clammy handshake as it often leaves the receiver with an uncomfortable feeling. No one ever wants to shake hands with someone who perhaps has dead fish handshake. It's quite unpopular & often taken to signify a weak character.

The knuckle grinder is the key trademark of the aggressive 'tough guy' type. Unfortunately, you just can't do much about it unless you're ready to go all out & hit the other person.

Like the palm-down thrust, the stiff-arm thrust often tends to be used by aggressive people who don't want to interact & its main purpose is to keep you at a distance & away from that person.

Rubbing the palms together

This's how people communicate positive anticipation. Imagine that you discuss an upcoming trip with someone & they start rubbing their palms together. You'll probably also notice that their eyes are also shining with delight, as they're very enthusiastic about what you're saying. On the other side, rubbing your palms together slowly might come across as creepy.

Rubbing the thumb against the fingers is also a common gesture employed by waiters or porters, etc. As a hint for tip. This's obviously a gesture that should be avoided at all times by a professional person when dealing with his or her clients.

Hands clenched together

Though initially this might seem like a confident gesture, it's actually a sign of frustration as the person is trying to hold back negative emotion. And like all negative gestures, something needs to be done to counteract this gesture or that person will perhaps remain locked in his negative emotions.

Hand to face gesture

Remember our previous discussion about how hiding our palms are also a gesture, which has been carried on from our childhood. This's somewhat the same thing. When we hear something unpleasant, we also tend to cover our ears. When we say something horrible or when we tell a lie, our hands unconsciously go to our mouth. This's much more noticeable in children because as we grow older, our gestures become subtler & less obvious. The hand to face gesture still remains though. It'll occur whenever someone's lying or exaggerating or trying to cover up something or simply hiding something.

Don't always assume that the next person is lying though whenever you witness this gesture but rather go on your guard because it does mean that something's up. Further observation of that person, his words & gestures as well as the surroundings will also let you know about whether to trust that person or not.

In contrast to the hand to face gesture, which usually signals deceit, the fingers in mouth gesture mean something different. It's done by people when they're tense or when they're in a stressful situation. It usually means that that person is seeking comfort.

Crossing arms

Hiding behind a barrier is a normal human response that we all learn at an early age to protect ourselves. As children, we hid behind objects, but as we grow older, we simply start folding our arms across our chest whenever threatening situations arise.

As we grow older, we also develop the arm crossing gesture to the point where it has become less clear to others & more difficult to pick up. Whenever someone's being defensive, they're likely to fold their arms firmly across their chest. There're many arm crossing techniques including the standard arm cross gesture, the reinforced arms cross, partial arm cross, arms gripping & disguised arm cross gestures. Almost all of them mean the same thing & a person is likely to do them in order to give themselves a feeling of security in uncomfortable situations.

Now let's look into other aspects..

What do breathing patterns reveal?

Secondly, we should also take a mental note of the other person's breathing patterns. You should try & look for cues regarding how they breathe so that you can match that in your mirroring process. Remember, although the other person might not be consciously aware of what you're doing, their subconscious will register this piece of information. As a result, the person you're speaking with will relate to you as a friendly presence. Some people simply breathe with their diaphragms whereas others breathe with their upper chests. This's a learned behavior, one that starts at birth. You might need to practice these breathing techniques so that it doesn't look unnatural when you adjust to match the person across from you.

What do energy levels reveal?

The energy levels of your conversation partner also gives indications about their personality. This information is vital in building rapport & you should pay close attention. Observe their demeanor. Does the other person seem like a bright & confident person? Or do they perhaps appear timid? Factor in this aspect of their personality before choosing a persona. Remember, in order to build rapport the other person needs to feel comfortable in your presence. Always be ready to adapt & adjust accordingly. If you ever seem aggressive or even out of sync with them, their subconscious will register this fact & your relationship will suffer.

What do speech patterns reveal?

And finally, we've to take into account the volume & tone of our voice. Because speech is your main mode of correspondence, you need to factor in this criteria the most. Try & mirror the speech patterns of your conversation partner. Search for answers to these questions when you're building rapport: Is the other person speaking in a low tone or are they more vocal? What kind of words do they choose, complicated or simple? How fast are they talking? If you find answers to these questions & mirror the other person accordingly, you'll find them more inclined to act positively towards you.

Chapter 23. How to Take Advantage Of Analyzing People

First things first, the word "manipulate" has quite a bad rap to it, but for the purpose of this section, I would like you to see that word in a different light. To help you see manipulation from a different perspective, consider the following examples:

Jack wants his friends to have a great evening at a party. He suddenly bumps into one of them, spilling their drink in the process. Jack smiles disarmingly and apologizes for the accident even though clearly it was the other person's fault. Both had a great evening.

Jill wants to make her work colleague look bad. She spreads negative rumors about the colleague. Eventually, the colleague gets to hear the rumors and feels sad and loses self-esteem.

In the first example, Jack manipulated his friend's feelings to make them feel better about a bad situation. In the second example, Jill manipulated her colleague's feelings to make them feel bad. The problem is not with the manipulation; instead, it is with the motive behind the manipulation.

Here's the message I am trying to get at from the above: to manipulate (in the context of this book) is to intentionally influence someone into changing their mind or behavior without any intent of causing harm to the other person. It is a mutually beneficial act—a win-win for all involved. "Fake it till you make it!" is a cliché that people use to motivate others to believe in themselves. This also holds true for body language. When you assume a body posture or a physical position or an attitude that you would like to have, your brain immediately begins to release hormones that make you actually feel that way!

Now that you clearly understand what I mean by faking your body language in order to manipulate others to do as you want, let me share with you two quick tips on how to fake it until you get the result you desire. I recommend that you should make a handful of videos of your verbal presentations in different situations. They don't necessarily have to be lengthy videos. When you play back the videos, turn off the sound so that you only see your body movements, gestures, and facial expressions. Observe what your body is saying. Does it say exactly what you mean? Is there a way you can make it convey the message you intend in a clearer way?

Few minutes before a meeting (in a social or professional setting), take deep breaths. Be present and mindful of your environment. Ensure that you take your attention off the meeting or whatever the near future holds and focus your attention on your present moment. This is a mindfulness practice. Steady yourself with deeper breaths. Clench and unclench your fists to make sure they are not shaky. All this will help you to become calmer when you eventually get into the meeting, and it will make you become more aware of your gestures and body movements.

Now, let us consider some of the practical ways to fake your body language properly so that you appear confident and interested in someone or make others comfortable around you even when you are not in the least any of these things!

Faking Interest

It is easy for anyone to tell you, "Show interest even when you are not." The problem with this advice is that the average person (who doesn't know how to fake their body language) is likely to become robotic in doing this. First of all, you need to understand that interest has a lot to do with the human attention span. And the normal human attention span doesn't last for long—at least not without some form of disinterest at some point or distraction. So, when you are faking interest in someone or something, here's how to do it.

You have to look like you are interested, but don't overdo it. Human beings don't have a 100% attention span to anything for a long time. So, when you show interest (or fake interest in other people), be sure to keep the show up for only about 70% of the time. Trying to fake interest in someone for longer periods will expose you as fake!

No one likes it when they are being "taken for a ride." Well, that is what it feels like when you want to get something from someone by faking interest in them. The poorest way to do this is by showing interest in someone just right before you ask them for a favor. For example, someone approaches you and offers you a compliment, and right after that, they go, "I was wondering if you could help me . . ." and they blurt out whatever it is they were really after. It doesn't take a genius to figure out that the earlier compliment given was not an honest one but a means to an end—the end, in this case, being the favor they want from you. So, if you want to compliment the person, that's fine, but make sure to give the compliment genuinely.

Discuss a variety of issues that will lead up to the favor you intend to ask. While this involves verbal communication, your body language throughout the interaction should show that you have a genuine interest in the issues or topics you talk about.

Making People Comfortable Around You

Closely linked to faking interest in people is learning how to make people comfortable being around you. If you can fake this successfully, you will be able to build a strong rapport with other people in a relatively short amount of time. Interestingly, while you may feel it is fake and unreal at the initial stages of using these techniques, with time, you will become so good at it that it no longer feels like faking. This is when you have moved from faking it to making it!

Mirroring: The Chameleon Effect

The chameleon effect is simply mirroring the other person's body language and speech pattern. Tuning yourself to reflect the other person back to themselves is a quick way to make them feel really comfortable around you and even like you in the process. When you mirror or mimic their sitting posture, tone of voice, gestures, body angle, expressions, and so on, you send an unconscious message to the other person that tells them you are like them in many ways. This makes them relax or let down their guard around you.

Conclusion

Be consistent in your words and non-verbal cues.

Speaking with another person, we influence him, whether we like it or not. Sometimes we do it intentionally, for example, when we are trying to piss off or cheer someone. Statements requiring a reaction may be as follows:

"You heard that ...", or

"This nasty Mel Gibson!", or "You know what happened ?!", or "I love you".

With our own statements, we can unconsciously cause a person to a variety of associations and reactions. For example, asking "How are you?" We never know what the answer will be. A person can take and pour out all his grief.

Our mood can also affect others. If we are happy, then everyone around us is also happy. We are sad—and others are sad too. Often we ask people to change:

"Get a hold of yourself!"

"Take it easy!"

In order to act more strongly, one must simultaneously with words produce actions convincing the interlocutor of the seriousness of your intentions. If you want to calm someone down, you should not take him by the shoulders and shake with a cry "When will you finally calm down?". To do this, you must first calm down yourself. Parents of babies understand how hard it is, but even with children, it works. "You must be tired," is the way to speak, accompanying the words with a yawn.

In this case, you need to radiate peace of mind, speak quietly, make smooth body movements, breathe evenly. To give someone confidence, you need to act

...fidently. Acting this way, you give the interlocutor's mind a hint, an example: you show with your appearance that it is possible to attain the desired state. There is a mutual understanding on a personal level. When you talk about something, you analyze; when you act, you create impressions, sometimes very strong. Think for yourself: would you prefer to talk about a kiss or get a kiss?

If your words mean one thing, and body language and voice mean another, the person will prefer to listen to the non-verbal message. If someone shouts "Calm down!", You will not listen to the words, but to the feelings that this cry will cause. It is unlikely that you calm down, rather, on the contrary, you get into a little more nervousness. To do this, do not even need to be able to read minds.

CPSIA information can be obtained
at www.ICGtesting.com
Printed in the USA
LVHW020912270521
688665LV00019B/1138

9 781667 129556